GUIDE SIGN GRAPHICS

©2006 PIE BOOKS

PIE BOOKS
2-32-4 Minami-Otsuka, Toshima-ku, Tokyo 170-0005 JAPAN
Tel: +81-3-5395-4811   Fax: +81-3-5395-4812
E-mail: sales@piebooks.com
        editor@piebooks.com
www.piebooks.com

ISBN4-89444-524-7 C3070
Printed in Japan

The designs used on the jacket were provided by:
BAUER-CONCEPT & DESIGN
EMOTIONAL SPACE DESIGN INC.
GOTTSCHALK+ASH INTERNATIONAL
KOTOBUKI CORPORATION
MINALE BRYCE DESIGN STRATEGY
NEWSOM DESIGN
REI DESIGN & PLANNINGS
RIAN IHARA DESIGN OFFICE
T. GLOVER CO., LTD.
THE McCULLEY GROUP

CONTENTS

FOREWORD

Neon signs that glow in the night sky, old-fashioned plaques on historical architecture, road and traffic signs, station information boards, billboards: all signs offering information that helps people along their way. We see a huge variety of signs everywhere in our daily lives. Recently, "barrier-free signs" implementing universal designs, such as Braille writing and sidewalk guideway lines, are on the rise, helping to create a barrier free society for all to enjoy. A "sign system" is set-up to design comprehensive signage that integrates such considerations required by this complex society. The sign system ensures that the signs not only provide information and guide the way, but also present the proper information in the proper place, making effective use of graphics, colors, and shapes.

The purpose of this publication is to serve as a reference for creators involved in flat or spatial design. This is a collection of not only Japanese works but also signage from all over the globe, resulting in a chance to see how signage is developed and implemented in other areas of the world. There has been very little published about this topic in recent years, thus the inclusion of works from a broad range of countries, including Brazil and Italy. You will find an exhaustive variety of patterns used in public, commercial, educational, medical, corporate, and exhibition facilities. In particular, you will find comprehensive sign systems for public facilities boasting features that provide information for all visitors, regardless of age, sex, nationality, etc.

Within this highly diversified display of sign systems, we introduce a multitude of superior guide-sign designs showing excellent application of multi-functions, effective expressions, and smooth transfer of essential information to the receiver.

Last but not least, we would like to thank all the wonderful creators that, despite their busy schedules, patiently cooperated with us and graciously provided excellent works to be included in this publication.

はじめに

夜空に光るネオンサイン、歴史的建造物に設置されたサイン、道路交通標識、駅の案内板、ショップ、看板など、人の行動を助ける "情報" を提供するサインは私たちの日常生活の様々な場所で目にすることができます。近年はユニバーサルデザインを重視した点字サインや誘導ブロックなどの、バリアフリーサインも注目されています。サインシステムとはそうした複数のサインを総合的にデザインすることをいいます。単に文字で情報を伝え、人々を目的地へ誘導するだけでなく、サインシステムにはグラフィック・ディスプレイ・色・形など、必要な場所に必要な情報が提供されることが必要とされます。

本書は平面や空間をデザインするクリエイターの方々が参考になるガイドサインを日本全国の作品だけでなく、注目に値する海外の作品も多く集めました。ブラジルやヨーロッパなどを含めた、広汎な国々の作品をまとめた本は近年にはなかったものです。また、コンテンツも公共・商業・教育・医療・企業・展示会施設など多様なパターンを網羅しました。そのなかでも「年齢や性別、国籍など不特定多数の人々が目にするサイン＝情報」である公共施設をより充実させました。

多種多様なサインシステムのなか、それぞれが持つ役割と機能をくみ取り、効果的に表現し、受け手に伝達していく優れたガイドサインデザインの数々をご紹介いたします。

最後になりましたが、忙しいなかご協力いただき、快く作品をご提供いただいたクリエイターのみなさまにこの場を借りてお礼を申し上げます。

EDITORIAL NOTES

Facility name, location　サイン設置 施設名・場所名

Description of sign location　サイン設置場所の詳細

Staff Credits　スタッフクレジット

Year of Completion　製作年

Explanation of signs and facility　サイン説明または施設説明

Abbreviation　略記号

CL: Client　クライアント
S: Supervisor　監修者
PR: Producer　プロデューサー
PC: Project Coordinator　プロジェクト・コーディネーター
DD: Design Director　デザイン・ディレクター
D: Designer　デザイナー
P: Photographer　フォトグラファー
DF: Design Firm　デザイン事務所
SCULPT: Sculptor　彫刻家
ART: Artist　アーティスト
CO: Construction　施工（製作）
AR: Architect　建築・設計
P(ss): Photographer (site shots)　実例写真撮影者
SB: Submitter　作品提供者

Full names of all others involved in the creation / production of the work.
上記以外の制作スタッフの呼称は略さずに記載しております。

Please note that some credit data has been omitted at the request of the submittor.
作品提供者の意向によりクレジット・データの一部を記載していないものがございます。

The first letter of all names written in English are capitalized, all other letters are lower-case.
英語名は頭文字のみ大文字、それ以外は小文字で表記統一しております。

The "kabushiki gaisha (K.K.)" and "yugen gaisha (Ltd.)" portions of all Japanese company name have been omitted.
各企業に付随する、"株式会社、(株)" および "有限会社、(有)" は表記を省略させて頂きました。

Customs House

Library ライブラリー

CL: City of Sydney
PC: Incoll
DD: Ray Parslow
D: Ray Parslow, Jacqueline Morony
DF, P(ss), SB: Frost Design, Sydney
CO: Central Signs
AR: Lacoste+Stevenson

AUSTRIA 2005

University College for the Creative Arts at Epsom and Farnham

Signage and way-finding graphics developed for the site of a modern library in one of Sydney's most important heritage buildings. It seemed only natural that the graphics be inspired by the act of reading: hence words appear to have jumped out of books onto the walls, doors, and floors, with letters coming together in unexpected ways. Slender wayfinding and identification poles suspended from the ceiling act as signposts at key locations. The exterior identification sign was conceived as a modern "obelisk", reflecting the coming together of old and new.

シドニーで最も古いビルの1つにある近代的図書館のサイン / 情報グラフィックス。"読むこと"から着想を得たデザインでは、本から飛びだした文字が壁・ドア・床上で思いがけない形に並んでいる。天井から下りる細長い柱は経路や施設を案内する標識として機能。現代のオベリスク*のような屋外サインは、新旧が共存するさまを反映したもの。* 古代エジプトの神殿に多く見られる記念碑の一種

Seattle Public Library

Library ライブラリー

CL: Office for Metropolitan Architecture
PC: Jim Shedden
D: Henry Cheung and Bruce Mau
DF, P, SB: Bruce Mau Design
AR: Rem Koolhaus

USA 1999

Referred to as a "big strong font made friendly", the new library's identity is based on a font whose easy readability endows it with a highly recognizable presence. Environmental graphics have been designed using an approach that equates "wordmark" with landmark, i.e. signage integrates with architecture through material and scale. Whimsical elements such as playful, oversized supergraphics and giant interior exterior "title" walls respond to the structural requirements and the needs of users, adults and children.

新しい図書館のサインは「フレンドリーにさせる印象的なフォント」がポイント。読みやすさが高い視認性を実現した。ランドマークの機能を備えた「ワードマーク」としてデザインされたサインは、素材とサイズにより建物と融合。特大グラフィックスや屋内外の巨大「タイトル」壁などは建物としての構造上の条件と年齢を問わない利用者のニーズを、同時に満たしている。

Katholische Kirche Vorarlberg

Church　教会

CL: Katholische Kirche Vorarlberg
PC, DD, D: Sigi Ramoser, Walter Buder
DF: Sägenvier Designkommunikation
SB: Sigi Ramoser

AUSTRIA 1999

The national headquarters building of the Catholic church. Office names appear behind the greeting, "Grüss Gott" ("Greet The Lord").

カトリック教会のオーストリア国内の総本部のためのサイン。「Grüss Gott (主よ、汝を迎える)」という挨拶のことばの後ろに施設の名称が見えるようになっている。

Halle F, Vienna

City Hall シティホール

CL: Wiener Stadthallen Gruppe, Vienna
S: Mr G. Feltl, Managing Director
DD: Justus Oehler
D: Christiane Weismüller, Justus Oehler
DF: Pentagram Design, Berlin
CO: Kahmann-Frilla, Austria
AR: dietrich | Untertrifaller Architekten
P(ss): J. Oehler   SB: Pentagram Design Ltd.

AUSTRIA 2006

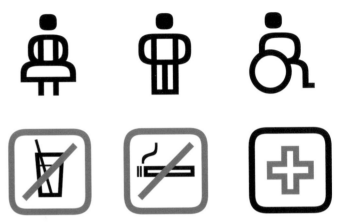

The brief was to design a signage/wayfinding system that would be visible but blend with the modern architecture and grey/red/natural wood finish interior. Elements were thus restricted to type and pictograms, applied directly to walls and doors using decals, to allow for future changes without damaging wall surfaces, at minimal cost. Eurostile Extended was chosen because it best reflects the architectural style of the building, and the pictograms designed to harmonize with the typeface. Outside a large, three-dimensional red rotating F signposts and advertises the new concert hall.

モダンな建築やグレー / 赤 / 無着色の木の内装にあう見やすいサインシステム・デザイン。要素を文字とピクトグラムに限定し、下地を傷つけず低コストで変更可能な転写式で壁とドアに直接表示した。フォントは建物によくあうEurostile Extended。ピクトグラムは文字にあわせてデザイン。屋外で回転する「F」の大型サインは新音楽堂を宣伝している。

Oita Pref. Drivers Licence Center
大分県運転免許センター

Drivers License Center 免許センター

CL: Oita Pref.　大分県
DD: Taro Watanabe (Emotional Space Design Inc.)　渡辺太郎（エモーショナル・スペース・デザイン）
D: Kiriko Watanabe (Emotional Space Design Inc.)　渡辺希理子（エモーショナル・スペース・デザイン）
P, SB: Emotional Space Design Inc.　エモーショナル・スペース・デザイン
CO: Kotobuki Corporation　コトブキ　AR, Design Partner: Kume Sekkei　久米設計

JAPAN 2006

Alphabetical signs were placed at fixed point to enable users to differentiate the location and purpose of three intertwining areas at a glance. Total design control was achieved by using the same design system for fittings throughout the facility. By painting the walls of the areas in different colors to assist in wayfinding, the sign system takes the stress out of searching.

混在する三つの目的別エリアを、利用者が一目で認知できるよう、アルファベットによる定点表示を実施。併せて施設内備品も同じシステムでトータルにデザインコントロールを行った。壁面をエリアカラーで塗り分けるなど、カラーによるウェイファインディングにより、"探すこと" のストレスを感じさせないサインシステムを行っている。

Yamanashi General Traffic Center
山梨県総合交通センター

General Traffic Center　総合交通センター

CL: Yamanashi Pref.　山梨県
DD: Taro Watanabe (Emotional Space Design Inc.)　渡辺太郎（エモーショナル・スペース・デザイン）
D: Ai Takaaki (Emotional Space Design Inc.)　高明 愛（エモーショナル・スペース・デザイン）
P, SB: Emotional Space Design Inc.　エモーショナル・スペース・デザイン
CO: Kotobuki Corporation　コトブキ　AR, Design Partner: Kume Sekkei　久米設計

JAPAN　2006

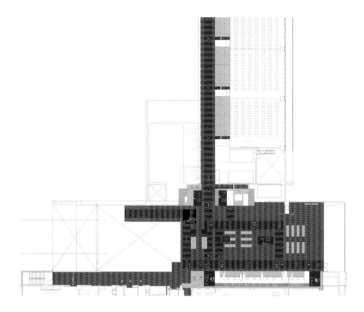

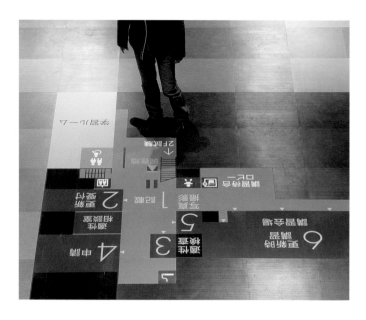

The object here was to develop a signage system to provide intellectual stimulation for the user, with spaces and signs forming a harmonious whole. To allow ease of movement between the levels of the facility, each of which have different functions, zebra crossings were applied to floors, helping users reach their destinations smoothly.

空間とサインが渾然一体となった、利用する人のインテリジェンスを喚起する装置としてのサイン計画を目指した。施設の階層が目的別に分かれているフロアの中で、スムーズに移動ができるよう、経路の床面に横断歩道を模したゼブララインでグラフィック処理。その上をたどっていくと順路に沿って目的地に到着できるようなシステムとした。

Saga Healthy Active Life Promote Center
佐賀市健康運動センター

Healthy Active Life Promote Center　健康運動センター

CL: Saga City　佐賀市
DD: Taro Watanabe (Emotional Space Design Inc.)　渡辺太郎（エモーショナル・スペース・デザイン）
D: Ai Takaaki (Emotional Space Design Inc.)　高明 愛（エモーショナル・スペース・デザイン）
P, SB: Emotional Space Design Inc.　エモーショナル・スペース・デザイン
CO: Kotobuki Corporation　コトブキ　AR, Design Partner: Kume Sekkei　久米設計

JAPAN 2004

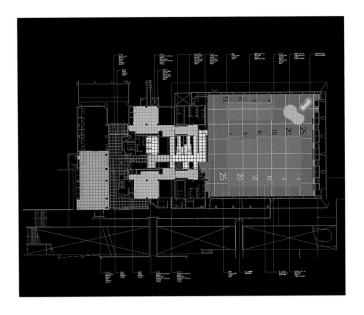

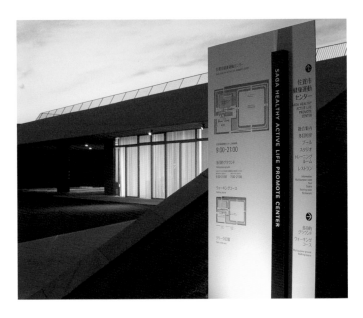

A grid pattern design modeled on a network of creeks was employed in homage to Saga Creek, a waterway that has sustained the people of Saga since ancient times. And by developing a conceptual narrative in which Saga Creek (the grid lines) flows into a large pool, the design not only acts as imagery, but performs zoning and guide functions as well.

遥か昔より佐賀の人々の生活を支えてきた佐賀クリークに敬意を表し、縦横無尽に流れるクリークをイメージしたグリッドパターンを施している。また、佐賀クリーク（グリッドライン）の終着が大きな水源（プール）に至るコンセプチュアルなストーリー展開で、イメージのみならずゾーニング及び誘導としての機能性も併せ持ったデザインとなっている。

Saitama Prefectual Budokan　埼玉県立武道館

Gymnasium　武道館

CL: Saitama Pref.　埼玉県
CO, SB: Kotobuki Corporation　コトブキ
AR: MHS Planners, Architects & Engineers　松田平田設計
P(ss): Nacása & Partners　ナカサアンドパートナーズ

JAPAN 2003

A simple building with a distinctive tension that pays homage to the marital arts tradition, yet hints at the development of a new tradition. Directional signs are also motifs to complement the architectural spaces. At the entrance to each arena, the facility name appears on a black sign against a red wall, making for signage that blends harmoniously with the architecture, yet is assertive in its own right.

武道の伝統を大切にしながら、次代への発展を感じさせるシンプルで独特の緊張感を持った建築物。誘導サインも建築空間に合わせ、隷書体の文字を使って伝統的なモチーフを取り入れた、シンプルなデザイン。各道場の入口には黒色の室名サインと、赤く塗装した壁面を組み合わせて設置し、建築に調和しながらも主張したサインとして機能させている。

所沢市提供

Tokorozawa Municipal Gymnasium　所沢市民体育館

Gymnasium　スポーツ施設

CL: Tokorozawa City　所沢市
S, DF: Hiromura Design Office　廣村デザイン事務所
CO, SB: Kotobuki Corporation　コトブキ
AR: Sakakura Associates Architects and Engineers　坂倉建築研究所
P(ss): Katsuhiko Murata (SS Tokyo Co., Ltd.)　村田雄彦（SS東京）

JAPAN　2004

男子トイレ
Men's Toilet
11-男

女子トイレ
Ladies' Toilet
11-女

多目的トイレ
Everybody Toilet
11-多

多目的トイレ
Everybody Toilet
11-多&オ

自販機コーナー
Vending Machine
11-目

喫煙所
Smoking Area
※11-煙
（※斜線部に割り付ける可能性あり。）

キッズコーナー
Kids Room
11-キ1.2

多目的体育室
Multi Purpose Gym
11-多体

卓球室
Table Tennis Room
11-卓

幼児体育室
Kids Training Room
11-幼

トレーニング室
Training Room
11-ト

下足スペース
Boot Cupboard
11-下

選手控室1-A
Athlete Room 1-A
11-選1-A

選手控室1-B
Athlete Room 1-B
11-選1-B

選手控室2-A
Athlete Room 2-A
11-選2-A

選手控室2-B
Athlete Room 2-B
11-選2-B

貴重品ロッカー
Baggage Lockers
11-貴

スポーツ情報ギャラリー
Sports Gallary
11-ス

会議室1-A
Conference Room 1-A
11-会1-A

会議室1-B
Conference Room 1-B
11-会1-B

会議室2-A
Conference Room 2-A
11-会2-A

会議室2-B
Conference Room 2-B
11-会2-B

給湯室
Hot-Water Supply
11-給

S=1/10

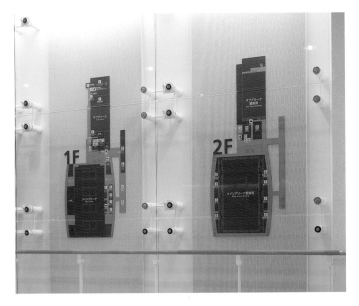

Sports facility used for major events such as the national athletic championships. Guide signs such as noticeboards and room names feature a uniform punched metal look, while original pictogram designs are sprinkled liberally throughout the facility, highlighting its unique character.

国体などの大規模な大会にも使われるスポーツ施設。ガイドサインは掲示板や室名など、パンチングメタルをベースに統一した。また、オリジナルのピクトデザインが豊富で、施設の個性を引き出している。

Kunimi Cultural Center Mahoroba
国見町文化会館「まほろば」

Cultural Center　文化会館

CL: Kunimi-cho　国見町
DD: Hiroyuki Yamada (T.Glover Co., Ltd.)　山田裕之（テイ・グラバー）
D: Noriko Fukano (T.Glover Co., Ltd.)　深野紀子（テイ・グラバー）
DF, CO, SB: T.Glover Co., Ltd.　テイ・グラバー
AR: Nihon Sekkei, Inc.　日本設計

JAPAN 2004

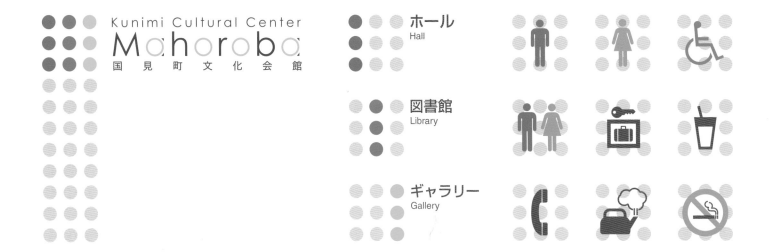

A graphical system based on dots, which had also been used as a motif in the architectural design, was considered in developing the signage program. The aim was a simple design that brings to life the messages on the signage. The aim was accenting spaces while giving functionality by allocating a specific color to each area. Applying the signage directly to the wall surfaces produced a feeling of synthesis between the architectural design and signage.

サイン計画は、建築でもモチーフとされているドット形状をポイントにグラフィックシステムを検討。サイン表示が生きるようなシンプルな意匠を心がけた。各エリアにテーマカラーを配することで、機能性を持たせつつ空間のアクセントになる事を目指した。また、壁面にサイン表示を直接施工する事で、建築とサインとの一体感が生まれた。

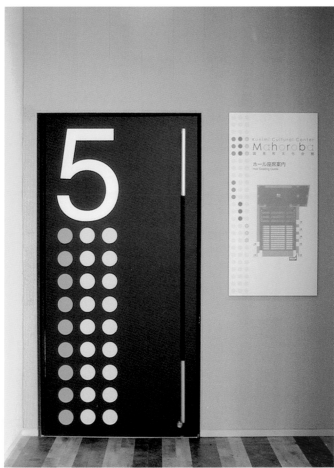

Kazusa Academia Hall　かずさアカデミアホール

Academia Hall　県立ホール

CL: Chiba Pref.　千葉県
S, AR: Sakakura Associates　坂倉建築研究所
DD, D: Taro Watanabe (while at Bikohsha Inc.)　渡辺太郎（びこう社 / 在職時）
P: Yuji Ishizuka　石塚勇二
CO: Bikohsha Inc.　びこう社
SB: Emotional Space Design Inc.　エモーショナル・スペース・デザイン

JAPAN 1999

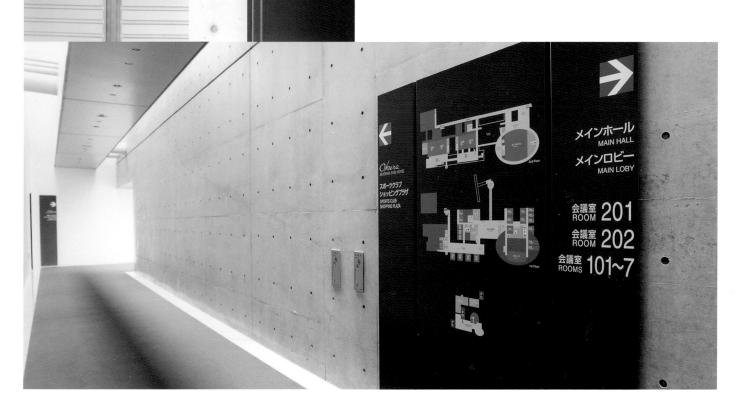

A full-scale conference center built in combination with a hotel. The center includes a main hall for a various uses, from international conferences to music concerts and other cultural events. The center offers a combination of small, medium and large conference rooms for academic conferences, seminars, exhibitions and other events, along with waiting rooms and reception rooms to make any event go smoothly and comfortably. Winner of the 9th Annual Public Buildings Association Prize.

ホテルも併設されている本格的なカンファレンスセンター。国際会議から音楽会などの文化活動まで、幅広い用途に対応できるメインホールがある。他にも学術会議、各種セミナー、展示会に利用できる大中小の会議室、細やかな心配りの行き届いた控室や応接室なども併設されている。第9回公共建築賞優秀賞を受賞。

Nonoichi Town Hall　野々市町新庁舎

Town Hall　町庁舎

CL: Nonoichi Town　野々市町
DD: Makoto Takeuchi　竹内 誠
D: Kan Minohara　蓑原 敢
DF, SB: Takeuchidesign Inc.　竹内デザイン
CO: Kajima, Magara, Chisansha, Izumi Joint Venture　野々市建築JV　鹿島・真柄・治山社・和泉・特定建設工事共同企業体
AR: Kohyama Atelier　香山壽夫建設研究所
P(ss): Mitsuru Goto　後藤 充

JAPAN 2005

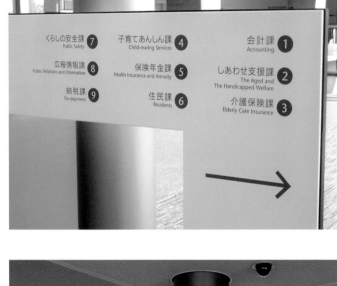

加賀五彩を使った色彩計画

石川県の伝統工芸には加賀友禅や九谷焼が有名である。それらの伝統工芸に共通して使われている色の種類は加賀五彩と呼ばれている。加賀五彩は、紅系統を生かした多彩調で、臙脂（えんじ）、藍、黄土、草、古代紫を基調としており、野々市町役場のサインには加賀五彩を意識したカラー計画を試みた。

臙脂	藍	黄土	草	古代紫
1F行政施設	2F行政施設	3F行政施設	情報交流施設	議会施設

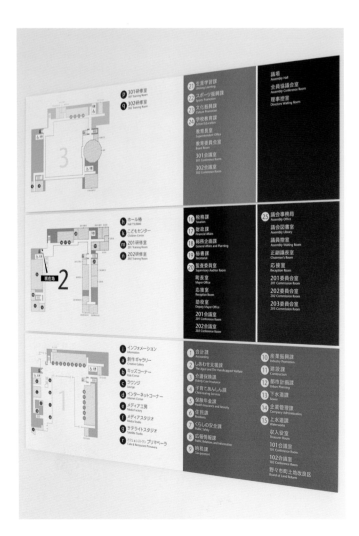

The new Nonoichi Town government office building: a U-shaped entrance overlooking the courtyard with an information exchange center on the right and an administration counter on the left. Signage was installed at this junction to provide wayfinding for visitors. Protruding signs, installed in the spacious counter area, can be seen even at a distance, identifying the different zones using the traditional "five colors of Kaga".

中庭に面しコの字型で構成され、エントランスを入ると右に情報交流館、左に行政窓口がある野々市市町新庁舎。サインは、この分かれ道を誘導する「道しるべ」として設置。一方、広い吹抜け空間を持つ行政窓口には、遠くからでもわかる突出しサインを設置した。また、「加賀五彩」といわれる加賀の伝統色がゾーニングカラーとして計画されている。

Kani Public Arts Center　可児市文化創造センターaLa

Arts Center　文化センター

CL: Kani-City (Gifu Pref.)　岐阜県可児市
DD: Makoto Takeuchi　竹内 誠
D: Norihiro Matsuo　松尾憲宏
DF, SB: Takeuchidesign Inc.　竹内デザイン
CO: NTT Facilities Inc.　NTTファシリティーズ
AR: Kohyama Atelier　香山壽夫建築研究所
P(ss): Mitsuru Goto　後藤 充

JAPAN 2002

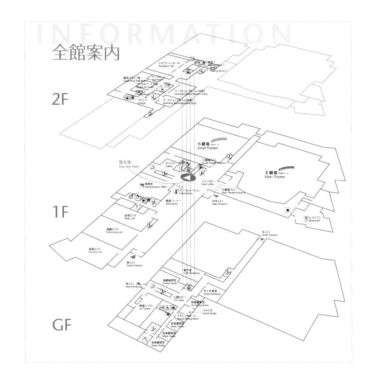

In the signage plan, materials such as corten steel and thick stainless steel plates were used without the fine finishing to capture the natural textures of the steel, copper, ceramic tiles, and wood. To ensure that information panels caught the eye, display cases were placed next to them. A deliberate effort was made to add visual rhythm to walls and actively draw attention to the presence of the signs.

サイン計画では、鉄、銅、タイル、木など素材感を生かし、建築の空間に存在を主張しつつも調和されるよう、耐候性鋼板やステンレスの厚板を素地の仕上のまま使用した。案内サインは空間の中での誘目性を確保するため、サインの隣に展示ケースをディスプレイ。壁面に視覚的なリズムを与え、積極的にサインの存在がアピールできるよう意識した。

Five Dock Library

Library ライブラリー

CL: City of Canada Bay
PC: Hans Gerber-Principal
D: Alex Papas
DF, SB: Minale Bryce Design Strategy
CO: A & W Signs
AR: Brewster Hjorth Architects
P(ss): Greg Bartley of Samiam Photo

AUSTRALIA 2004

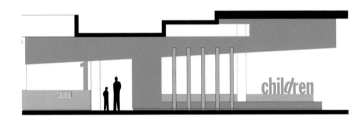

A system of environmental graphics serves as wayfinding devices and communicates the library's visual identity. The system uses a combination of dynamic and controlled elements, designed and placed to identify and direct, but also punctuate and complement the architecture. Identification of the library's various sections and open spaces is achieved with large fabricated numerals juxtaposed against various architectural elements. Colors both contrast and maintain a visual hierarchy, with color and form blending into the architectural fabric for a subtle, less invasive effect.

VIと経路案内の両機能をもつ図書館の環境グラフィックス。大胆だが抑制のきいたデザイン要素の組みあわせがガイド機能を発揮しつつ建築をひきたてている。館内のあちこちで数字のオブジェが色々な建築要素に添えられている。色彩はコントラストをきかせつつ視覚的優先順位を明確に表現。全体に色と形が主張しすぎない繊細なムードで建物に融合している。

Sasaguri Town Office　篠栗町役場

Town Office　町役場

CL: Sasaguri Town Office　篠栗町役場
S, PR, PC, CO: Yukinobu Yogi (Hadakogeisha)　与儀幸信（ハダ工芸社）
DD, D, P, P(ss), SB: Hitomi Ishikawa (Hadakogeisha)　石川ひとみ（ハダ工芸社）
DF: Hadakogeisha　ハダ工芸社

JAPAN 2005

A town blessed with nature; forests and greenery cover over 70% of the land. Utilizing this environment, trees are used as graphics in the signage system. The base color of green changes with each message type and is used in gradations throughout. The four accent colors were designed with the appeal of the four seasons - spring, summer, autumn, and winter - in mind.

町の70％以上が森林＝緑に恵まれた町。そうした環境を生かし、サインシステムでは森林の木々をグラフィックで表した。各係表示は基本色の「緑」色の変化による、全体的なグラデーションで表現している。また、4色のポイントカラーは春夏秋冬の楽しい四季を念頭に置いてデザインした。

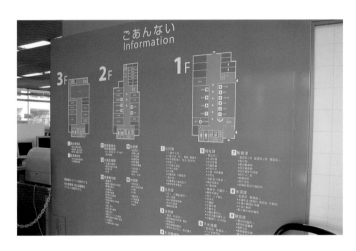

Toyota City: area around stations　豊田市内（駅周辺）

Station Plaza　駅周辺広場

CL: Toyota City　豊田市
DF: PAS Project Co., Ltd.　PAS計画
CO, SB: Kotobuki Corporation　コトブキ
AR: Ishimoto Architectural & Engineering Firm, Inc.　石本建築事務所
P(ss): Tokuaki Takimoto　滝本徳明

JAPAN 2005

A sign plan based on a barrier-free configuration created from a universal design aspect to meet the needs of all users, including the elderly, the disabled, and foreigners. In addition to displaying maps, the integrated sign system provides Braille guidance, voice guidance, and lighted guidance using LED panels.

高齢者、障害者、外国人などの利用をふまえ、ユニバーサルデザインの視点からバリアフリーの基本構想に基づいたサイン計画。総合サインには地図表示のほか、点字案内、音声案内、LEDによる電光案内が設置されている。

Kagoshima-Chuo Station　鹿児島中央駅

Station plaza　駅前広場

CL: Kagoshima City　鹿児島市
CO, SB: Kotobuki Corporation　コトブキ
P(ss): Tokuaki Takimoto　滝本徳明

JAPAN 2004

The station, built for the launch of the Kyushu Shinkansen bullet train service, was upgraded to serve as the overland gateway to Kagoshima. Bus stops were centered on the station for convenient passenger connections to other modes of transportation. Care was taken to make "barrier-free" directional signs to fit all traveler needs. Local attractions and specialties are also introduced, such as the monuments in front of the station and the traditional Satsuma kiriko cut glassware.

九州新幹線の一部開業に伴い整備された駅で、鹿児島の陸の玄関としてリニューアル。駅前にバス停を集めることで、交通機関の相互乗り継ぎの利便性を充実させた。誘導サインにはバリアフリーのための配慮はもちろんのこと、駅前にあるモニュメントや地元の伝統的工芸品である薩摩切子の紹介などもされている。

Yachimata Station, North Exit Station Plaza
八街北口駅前広場

Station plaza 駅前広場

CL: Yachimata City　八街市
DF: Yachimata City, Kotobuki Corporation　八街市　コトブキ
CO: Seiwa Kogyo, Kotobuki Corporation　聖和興業　コトブキ
SB: Kotobuki Corporation　コトブキ
P(ss): Tokuaki Takimoto　滝本徳明

JAPAN 2005

At present, as part of the town-planning project centered on the city of Yachimata, efforts are underway to develop an area that will become "the old hometown". The idea is to give people a feel for the natural features of Yachimata, as expressed in the directional signs, lighting, etc., positioned at the station and throughout the station plaza, using the local oyaishi stone as the unifying motif.

現在、八街市を中心とした区画整理に伴い「ふるさとの顔」となる街づくりが進められている。「八街の風土が感じられる街」をテーマに、誘導サイン、照明などが駅と駅前広場全体に広がり、大谷石をモチーフとしたデザインでまとめられている。

Kannai · Kangai Areas　関内・関外周辺地区

Public Street　公道

CL: Yokohama City　横浜市
DD: Kazuo Tanaka　田中一雄
D: Norihiko Hibiya (while at GK Sekkei Inc.), Toshihiko Irie, Tomomi Kimura　日比谷憲彦（在職時）　入江寿彦　木村友美
Map Design: Infogram　インフォグラム
DF: GK Sekkei Inc.　GK設計
CO, SB: Kotobuki Corporation　コトブキ
AR: Pacific Consultants Co., Ltd.　パシフィックコンサルタンツ
P(ss): Shigeru Ohno, Kazuo Tanaka　大野 繁　田中一雄

JAPAN 2002

Signs specifically designed for pleasant strolls throughout Yokohama, an internationally renowned tourist city. The main point was to introduce voice guidance signs, as well as interactive signs, while using contrasts and color schemes in graphics to assist visitors with reduced vision. Large arrow signs are implemented to make place names more noticeable.

国際観光都市、横浜を楽しく散策できるよう設置されたサイン。主要拠点には音声誘導サインや触知サインを導入し、グラフィックにも弱視者に配慮したコントラストや配色を使用。また、主要な目的地名が目に留まるよう矢羽サインが併設されている。

Imazu-cho Surroundings　今津町周辺地区

Public Street　公道

CL: Takashima City　高島市
DF, CO, SB: Kotobuki Corporation　コトブキ
P(ss): Shigeru Ohno　大野 繁

JAPAN 2005

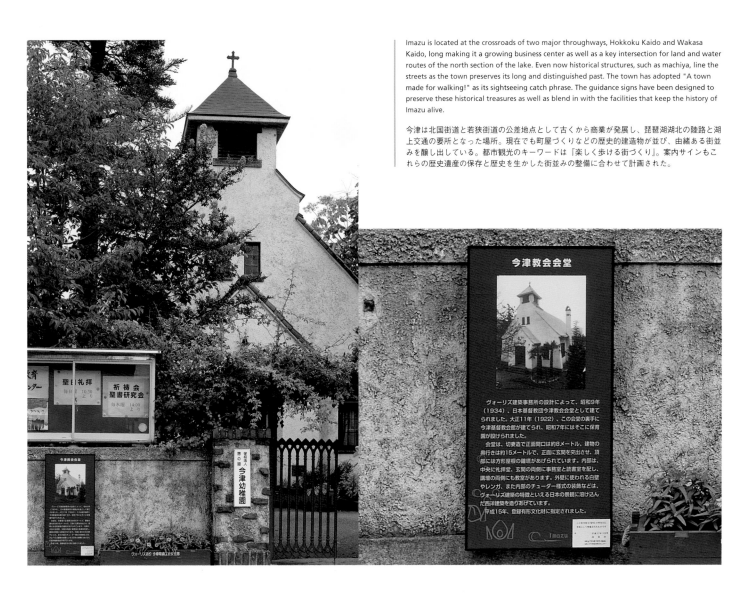

Imazu is located at the crossroads of two major throughways, Hokkoku Kaido and Wakasa Kaido, long making it a growing business center as well as a key intersection for land and water routes of the north section of the lake. Even now historical structures, such as machiya, line the streets as the town preserves its long and distinguished past. The town has adopted "A town made for walking!" as its sightseeing catch phrase. The guidance signs have been designed to preserve these historical treasures as well as blend in with the facilities that keep the history of Imazu alive.

今津は北国街道と若狭街道の公差地点として古くから商業が発展し、琵琶湖湖北の陸路と湖上交通の要所となった場所。現在でも町屋づくりなどの歴史的建造物が並び、由緒ある街並みを醸し出している。都市観光のキーワードは『楽しく歩ける街づくり』。案内サインもこれらの歴史遺産の保存と歴史を生かした街並みの整備に合わせて計画された。

Odawara Station, West Exit Station Plaza
小田原駅西口駅前広場

Station plaza 駅前広場

CL: Odawara City　小田原市
DF: PAS Project Co., Ltd.　PAS計画
CO, SB: Kotobuki Corporation　コトブキ
P(ss): Tokuaki Takimoto　滝本徳明

JAPAN 2004

Guide signs for the city are based on a sign manual, unifying the design, color and display style, which helps the signs blend in naturally with the historical flavor of the town.

市内の案内サインは、サインマニュアルに基づき、デザインや色、表示などが統一され、歴史の街に相応しい景観を形成している。

Niigata City Downtown　新潟市中心市街地

Public Road　公道

CL: Minisity of land, Infranstructure and Transceport Hokuriku Regional Developement Bureau, Niigata National Roads　国土交通省 北陸整備局 新潟国道事務所
DF, AR: Kaihatsugiken Co., Ltd.　開発技建
CO: Toa Doro Kogyo Co., Ltd.　東亜道路工業（施工）
CO, SB: Kotobuki Corporation　コトブキ（製作）
P(ss): Tokuaki Takimoto　滝本徳明

JAPAN 2005

Sign installations from the front of Niigata Station toward the Bandai District. The dark gray hue of the lampposts and other signs maintains the distinctive and classic characteristics of the symbol of Niigata, Bandai Bridge. The "talking signs" transmit the current position of a pedestrian carrying the "Signeido" receiver as he or she approaches a transmitter. In addition, signs are written in English, Spanish, Chinese, Korean, and Russian.

新潟駅前から万代地区にかけて行われたサイン整備。照明などもダークグレーの色調にすることで、新潟のシンボル「萬代橋」の風格あるイメージと一体となった景観を実現。音声案内は発信器の「シグネイド」を持ってサインに近づくと、音で現在地を知らせてくれる。また、表記は英語、スペイン語、中国語、ハングル、ロシア語を併記。

Gifu City Downtown　岐阜市中心市街地

Public Street　公道

CL: Gifu City　岐阜市
PR: Urban Design Center. Japan　財団法人都市づくりパブリックデザインセンター
DD: Toshihiko Kitayama　北山利彦
D: Toshihiko Irie, Shota Mitsuyasu, Sumito Kohno, Ayako Saito　入江寿彦　光安正太　功能澄人　斎藤絢子
DF, SB: GK Sekkei Incorporated　GK設計
P(ss): Toshihiko Irie　入江寿彦

JAPAN 2005

The wayfinding signage for Gifu City expresses the essence of Gifu through lighting and color while harmonizing with the charming streetscapes. The aim was symbolic design that represents the characteristics of Gifu City. Portable maps incorporating the same signage designs were also created, enabling tourists to traverse the city easily.

岐阜市の誘導サインは、魅力ある街並みと調和しながら、照明と色彩によって岐阜らしさを表現。岐阜市の個性を引き立たせる象徴的なデザインを目指した。また、サインと同じデザインでハンドマップを作成し、観光客がわかりやすく街をまわれるように配慮した。

Matsumoto City Downtown　松本市中心市街地

Public Street　公道

CL: Matsumoto City　松本市
PR: Isao Miyazawa　宮沢 功
PC: Toshihiko Kitayama　北山利彦
DD: Takenori Suda　須田武憲
D: Sumito Kohno　功能澄人
DF, SB: GK Sekkei Incorporated　GK設計

JAPAN 2005

Signage for the historic castle town of Matsumoto. Signs located around the castle have a light and airy design with wood posts to harmonize with scenery, while signs in the downtown area have a slab-like form and are made of stone to match the more solid storehouse architecture. Large highly legible typography is based on principles of universal design. The system strives to identify all public facilities, sightseeing spots, private facilities and more to be as useful as possible for users.

歴史的文化財が残る城下町、松本市。松本城周辺では景観に調和するよう木を柱とする軽快なデザインを、町中では蔵など重厚な造形に調和する石を用いた板状のデザインを施した。標示はユニバーサルデザインの観点から、書体や文字を大きく読みやすくした。また、公共施設や観光名所、民間施設など出来る限り掲示することで、利用者の利便性の向上を図った。

City of Brussels

Public Street 公道

CL: City of Brussels
S, PC: Jacques Bodelle
PR, DF, SB: ÉO Design Partners s.a.
DD: Jacques Bodelle, Chantal Veys
D: Christine Maniet, Alasdair Grant
CO: Adshel. J. C. Decaux
P(ss): Serge Verheylewegen, Eric Masquelier, Bastin-Evrard

BELGIUM (Still Under Production)

This project is still in development and production, 10 years after its initiation! The project includes global research concerning street furniture (bus shelters, benches, bins, street lighting, street nameplates, bicycle parking), public parking notices, including availability, museum entrances (for 96 museums!), local information about National Heritage buildings and sites, and finally, a pedestrian wayfinding system (a system intended for motorists was impossible to implement due to size).

この計画は開始後10年が経過した現在も開発・製作段階にある。計画では街路備品、美術館など96ヶ所の空き地、国家遺産に指定されている建物や場所、歩行者ウェイファインディングシステムに関する大規模な調査を実施。フランス語とオランダ語での標示は必須で、しかも英語およびドイツ語の需要もあったため計画は極めて困難だった。

Bullring

Public Street　公道

CL: Hammerson UK Properties
DD: David Hillman
D: Deborah Osborne
DF: Pentagram Design
SB: Pentagram Design Ltd.

UK 2003

This comprehensive, branded and integrated signage program includes: identification for external areas and entrances; wayfinding; information and directories within the main retail area; and signage for car parks. The system incorporates a bold, modern graphic language, presenting information with optimum clarity at key locations. Pictograms identify utilities, while the wayfinding system employs a series of large directional arrows on floors and walls. In the car parks, large typography greets visitors and bids them farewell, with prominent red arrows identifying Help Points.

屋外、エントランス、経路、ショッピング・エリア、駐車場等を案内する総合的サインプロジェクト。明瞭かつモダンにデザインされたサインが主要な場所をわかりやすくガイド。各施設はピクトグラムで表され、床や壁に描かれた大型の矢印が経路を案内。駐車場は大きな文字で案内され、ヘルプ・ポイントの位置が赤い矢印で示されている。

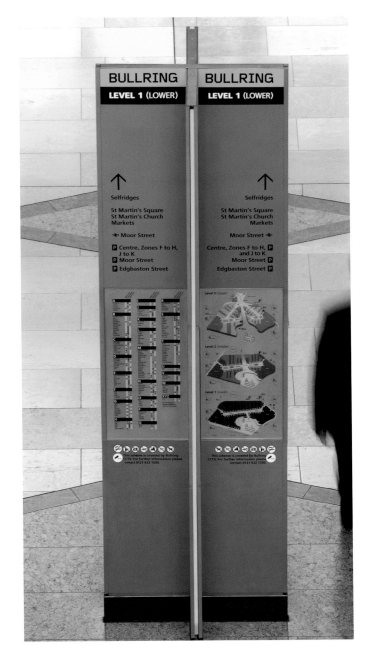

Town Center Tour

Public Street　公道

CL: City of Tournai
S, PC: Jacques Bodelle
PR, DF, SB: ÉO Design Partners s.a.
DD: Jacques Bodelle, Chantal Veys
D: Alasdair Grant, Christine Maniet, Corinne Demaet, Véronique Rappez
SCULPT: Christine Jongen
ART: Alasdair Grant
CO: Jean Vandervelde s.p.r.l.　P(ss): Yvan Glavie

BELGIUM 2004

Sign Design Society 2005 Grand Prix Award Winner. Tourenai, an ancient city located near the French border, was well preserved throughout the 20th century as it was far from the main highways linking Belgium to France. Its historical center, with a cathedral, city hall and medieval facades required materials and typography adaptive to the environment: wood poles, cast-molded figurines representing the old craftsmen, and cotton banners with typography and illustrations to match.

2005年サインデザイン協会大賞受賞。フランス国境に近いトゥルネイ市は、数百年間にわたって保存されてきたベルギーの古都。大聖堂、市役所、中世都市の外観を残したこの歴史の中心地は環境に適した材料やタイポグラフィーの使用を追求。そのためタイポグラフィーやイラストと同様に木製の電柱、昔の職人組合や木綿の旗を表す置物を使用した。

City of Albuquerque Downtown

Public Street　公道

CL: City of Albuquerque, New Mexico Transit Department
S: Richard Kuhn
PR: Clip Wyly
PC: Jamie Jett Walker
DD, D: Rick Vaughn, Lance Wyman
DF: Vaughn Wedeen Creative
CO: Health Sign Company
P(ss): Chip Wyly, Lance Wyman, Rick Vaughn　SB: Rick Vaughn

USA　2002

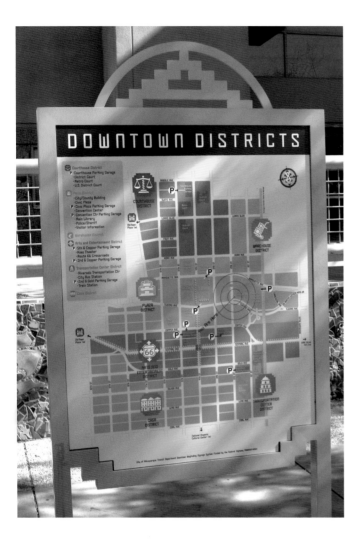

The Downtown Albuquerque Wayfinding Signage System comprises branding elements and directional information infused with the vibrant color and classic forms of New Mexico and the distinctive landmarks of the City of Albuquerque. It is designed to show the way to downtown destinations within each unique district, making the trip more enjoyable for tourists and residents. The signage program consists of: vehicular directional signs, street signs, pedestrian signs, parking signs, and district orientation maps on kiosks and parking garage walls.

アルバカーキ・ダウンタウン地域のウェイファインディング標示システム。ニューメキシコ特有の鮮やかな色合いと伝統的な形式を取り入れた方向標示で構成した。標示システムはディストリクト区域内の目的地を特定し、そこに至る方法を明確に表示するようデザイン。ダウンタウンの区域を区別して旅行者および住民に見やすく楽しめるよう工夫した。

Downtown Baltimore

Public Street 公道

PC: David Gibson
DD: Anthony Ferrara
D: Chris Griggs, Dominic Borgia
SB: Two Twelve Associates

USA 2002

Creating an identity for downtown Baltimore that captures what the area is all about and helps distinguish it from the larger, sprawling city surrounds. The identity was based on the Downtown Partnership's theme: Live, Work, Play. The program begins with a logo and slogan that captures the flavor of the historic and engaging locations. The downtown areas are distinguished by a specific building, each of which is represented in the overall downtown logo. The selected colors complement the existing vehicular signage, a well-known, functional system.

地域の全てを紹介しつつ周辺との差別化も図っているボルチモア市繁華街のサイン。デザイン・コンセプトは繁華街の組合のテーマでもある「生きる、働く、遊ぶ」。プロジェクトは魅力的な歴史ある街を表すロゴと標語作りから開始。各区域の特徴的建物が統一したロゴで案内されている。色は、機能性の高さで有名な既存の交通標識にあわせられた。

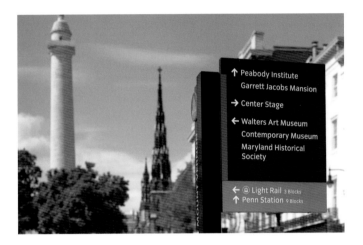

Kansas City

Public Street 公道

CL: City of Kansas City, Missouri
PC, D: Stacey Griffith
DD: Robert Brengman, Stacey Griffith
DF, SB: Corbin Design
CO: Interstate Highway Sign Corp., Little Rock, AR
P(ss): Matt McCormick

USA 2005

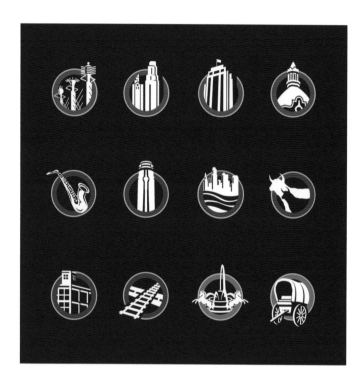

This vehicular and pedestrian wayfinding system is based on the image of a bull's-eye. Each wayfinding district falls within one of three concentric circles radiating out from the city's center. Districts in each circle are identified by color-red for the Downtown Core, green for the Greater Downtown, and blue for outlying districts. District icons-from the profiles of architecturally significant structures that represent serveral areas to the saxophone that stands for 18th and Vine's historic jazz venues-were drawn from the local culture. Signs within each destrict announce one's arrival and point the way to specific destinations and nearby parking. Pedestrian maps show the neighborhood and its destinations and parking areas.

的をイメージしたデザインの車両 / 歩行者用道案内システム。ダウンタウンの各区域は同心円の3色で表示。赤は中心部、緑は全域、青は周辺区域を表す。区域を識別するアイコンは地域文化の特徴を参考にした。区域内の表示は当区域に入ったことを表し、目的地や近隣駐車場への進路を示す。また、歩行者用マップは近隣の地理や目的地、駐車場がわかる仕組み。

Downtown Oklahoma City

Public Street 公道

CL: City of Oklahoma City, Missouri
PC: Mary Lou Pieth
DD: Jeff Corbin
D: Tony LaPorte
DF, SB: Corbin Design
CO: J & B Graphics, Oklahoma City, OK
P(ss): Matt McCormick

USA 2005

This unified wayfinding system for a two-square-mile section of the city's downtown replaced a hodgepodge of dissimilar signs. The system's art deco motif reflects downtown architecture. Visitors are directed to key downtown destinations including the site of the 1995 Alfred P. Murrah Building bombing, now the Oklahoma City National Memorial. Also included are destinations in Bricktown, a converted warehouse district that is home to a ballpark and restaurants, as well as the city's arts district and other entertainment venues. Trailblazer signage is designed to increase pedestrian traffic to areas including the memorial, Bricktown, and arts districts.

ダウンタウン面積2平方マイルの統一ウェイファインディング・システム。アールデコ風のモチーフは地域独自の建築を反映。1995年の連邦ビル爆破現場や野球場、レストランが集まる倉庫街を改造したブリックタウン、オクラホマ・シティのアート地区、その他の娯楽地区など、主要目的地に誘導。標示はこれらの地域への歩行者数を増やすよう設計した。

Walsh Bay

Public Street 公道

CL: Walsh Bay Redevelopment
PC: Steven Joseph
DD: John Spatchurst
DF, P(ss), SB: Spatchurst
AR: HPA Architects

AUSTRALIA 2004

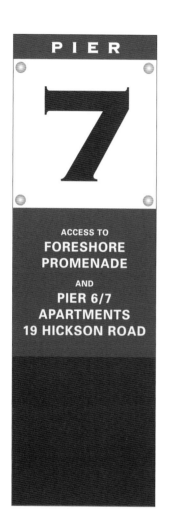

Walsh Bay is an industrial and maritime precinct on Sydney harbour. The redevelopment combined entertainment, residential and commercial facilities.

ウォルシュ・ベイはシドニーハーバーに位置する工業・海洋業地区。再開発は娯楽施設、居住区、商業施設を合わせて計画された。

Chicago City

Public Street 公道

PC: David Gibson
DD: Anthony Ferrara
D: Yanira Hernandez, Dominic Borgia
SB: Two Twelve Associates

USA 1998

A new design standard for all public signs on the streets of Chicago. Five pilot neighborhoods were identified for the study and the implementation of new standards, upon which a manual was developed that sets guidelines and policy standards for the overall system. This document will allow the city to continue to implement and maintain the program in the future. The essential components of the public signage program include parking regulations, street identifications, special destinations, cultural attractions, public and commercial transportation and neighborhood signs.

シカゴ市の全街路用公共サインを対象とした新デザイン基準。本プロジェクトを今後、継続的に実行するための礎となる、全システムのガイドラインと方針を定めたマニュアルが、5つの試験地域で新しい基準を研究・検証しながら開発された。この事業の必須要素には駐車規制 / 街路 / 観光地 / 文化催事 / 公営・民営交通機関 / 近隣地域のサインがある。

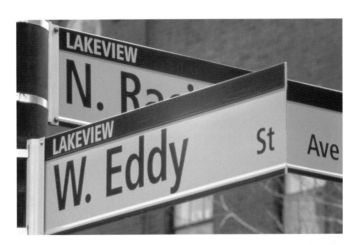

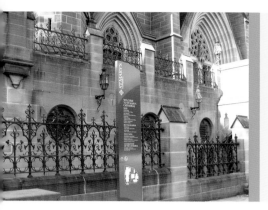

St. Mary's Cathedral, Australia

Cathedral 大聖堂

CL: St. Mary's Cathedral
PC: Romaine Teahan
DD: Steven Joseph
D: Nicky Hardcastle
DF, P(ss), SB: Spatchurst

AUSTRALIA 2005

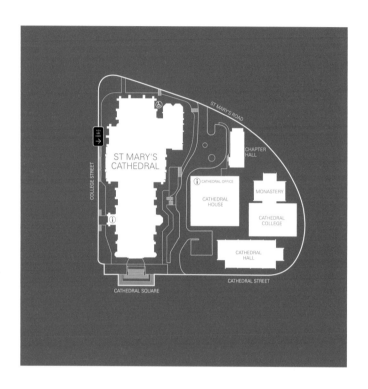

St. Mary's Cathedral is an important heritage building, in a prominent location, and plays a major role in the history of the Catholic Church in Australia. It attracts a great many tourists and visitors as a venerable place of prayer. The task was to create a signage system that reflects the importance and dignity of the Cathedral, and improves access to the Cathedral and to its history. The type, quantity and location of signage were therefore conceived to be iconic, functional and minimal.

セントメアリー大聖堂はオーストラリアのカトリック教会史上重要な役割を果たしてきた、街の中心に位置する歴史的建造物。崇高なイメージを保ちながら訪問客を大聖堂やその歴史へと、よりスムーズに誘導するサインシステムを制作。アイコニック、機能的、シンプルというコンセプトのもとサインの形態・設置数・場所が考案された。

Penn South

Public Street 公道

CL: Mutval Redevelopment Houses Inc.
D: L. Richard Poulin, Dovglas Morris
DF, SB: Poulin+Morris Inc.
P(ss): Various

USA 2002

Penn South is a large-scale residential complex covering ten-square blocks in Manhattan's Chelsea district originally built in the 1950's. Major renovations in 2002 included a comprehensive graphics and a wayfinding signage program unifying all of the various buildings, ancillary structures, and outdoor common spaces. The program also reinforces a new identity for the complex as a whole, joining the once disparate parts in to a single residential neighborhood.

ペン・サウスはマンハッタンのチェルシー地区に1950年代に建てられた10街区にまたがる巨大な共同住宅。2002年の大規模な改修工事で様々なビル、付属の建造物、屋外共有スペースの全てを統合する、包括的グラフィックス・案内サイン・プロジェクトが実施された。同時に新しいVIも強化され、ばらばらだった共同住宅に一体感を与えた。

Asturian Prerromanasque Welcome Center

Welcome Center 文化施設

CL: Principality of Asturias Government
DD, D: José Santamarina
DF, SB: Santamarina Diseñadores

SPAIN 2005

Wayfinding signage identifying the welcome center and sites of the preRomanesque Asturian monuments, San Miguel de Lillo and Santa Maria del Naranco.

スペイン、アストゥリアス地方にあるプレロマネスク様式の記念建造物、聖ミゲル・デ・リリョ王室礼拝堂と聖マリア・デル・ナランコ聖堂と、その観光センターを案内するためのサイン。

La Malva Botanical Park

Botanical Park　森林公園

CL: Hidrocantábrico
DD, D: José Santamarina
DF, SB: Santamarina Diseñadores

SPAIN 2000

Communication signage for a regional forest identifying the different botanical species.

様々な植物の種類を説明するため森林に設置されたサイン。

Virginia Avenue Park

Park　公園

CL: City of Santa Monica, California
S: Karen Ginsburg
PR: Karman Ltd.
PC, D: Lucy Gonzalez
DD: Carol Newsom
DF, SB: Newsom Design
AR: Koning Eizenberg Architecture
P(ss): Gonzalez / Newsom

USA　2005

A 5.82-acre park with facilities for youth, families and seniors, also home to a weekly farmer's market, an outdoor children's swimming pool, a new children's playground and green space for informal ball games, picnics and community events. The sign program covered all exterior and interior signs as well as interior photographic wall panels. The designers also created an identity symbol for the park and all printed promotional items.

子供、家族、老人向け設備が整い、週に一度の農産物直売、児童用屋外プール、運動広場、非公式球技場、ピクニックや地域イベントのためのスペースを備えた約2万3千平方メートルある公園のサインプロジェクト。屋内外用サインや屋内用写真壁パネルが制作された。それに伴い、公園のシンボルや宣伝用印刷物もデザインされた。

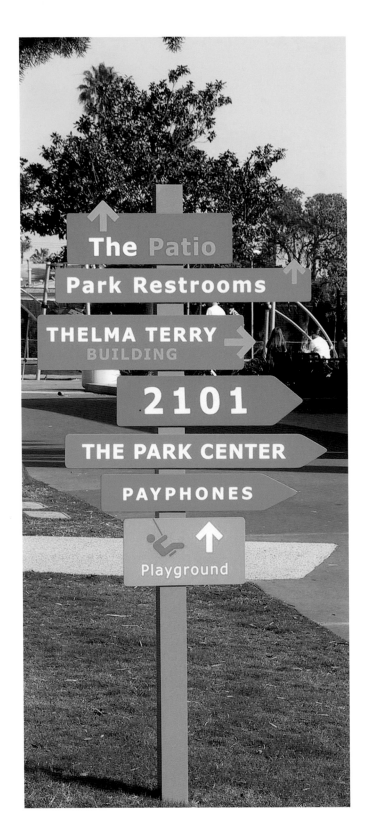

Shiodome SIO-SITE　汐留シオサイト公共地区

Public Street　公道

CL: Tokyo Metropolitan Government, Shiodome District Conference　東京都　汐留地区街づくり協議会
CO: Kotobuki Corporation, Hoankogyo Co., Ltd., Hoan Supply Co., Ltd.　コトブキ　保安工業・保安サプライ
DD, S: Shiodome District Conference・Urban Design Institute　汐留地区街づくり協議会・都市環境研究所
AR: Todec Inc.　トデック
P(ss): Katsuhiko Murata (SS Tokyo)　村田雄彦（SS東京）
SB: Kotobuki Corporation　コトブキ

JAPAN 2004

The Tokyo Metropolitan Govt. and Shiodome District Redevelopment Conference created a comprehensive environmental structure providing a community-centered system to maintain public facilities, including signage. The five districts of the Shiodome SIO-SITE area each have a theme color for signboards and street lighting; a design concept to create simple and esthetically harmonious signs. Greenery lining the streets blends in with the signage to create a flowing atmosphere, and the color-themed information boards work as great eye catchers with a logo that creates a feeling of belonging throughout the area.

東京都と汐留地区街づくり協議会は、総合的な環境形成を目指し、サインを含む公共施設整備・管理について協働体制をとっている。汐留シオサイトエリアは、1区から5区という5つの街で構成され、テーマカラーがサインボードと街路照明に施されている。デザインコンセプトは、わかりやすく、街に溶け込むサイン。街路の緑がサインに映り込むことで街路空間と一体となり、街の愛着を日々感じることができる。

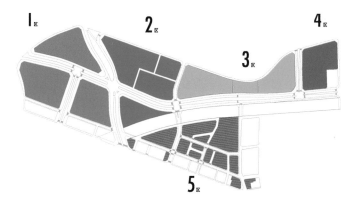

1区：WATER BLUE（5元素の一つ「水」を表現。シオサイトに接する海のイメージ。）
2区：LIGHT GREEN（鮮やかな「木」を表現。樹木の多い公園都市シオサイトに欠かせない色。）
3区：FLAME YELLOW（「火」から生まれた炎の色。人を包み込むパワーとあたたかさをもつ色。）
4区：EARTH BROWN（「土」の象徴。落ち着いた、人を和ませる色で、生活のステージを表現。）
5区：URBAN METAL（「金」すなわち金属を代表する。シオサイトの未来性を感じさせる色。）

Pampulha's Lake

Lake Park 公園

CL: Belo Horizonte City Hall
DD: Mariana Hardy & Fernando Maculan   D: Fernando Jorge da Silva, Gustavo Brasileiro, Laura Barbi, Márcio Barbalho
Design Assistants: Alexandre Perocco, Alice Vasconcellos, Ana Bárbara Ivo, André Coelho, Antonio Valladares, Bruno Teixeira, Carolina Salgado, Cássia Perocco, Cecília Rocha, Danilo Queiroz, Eduardo de Almeida, Gabriela Abdalla, Joana Carneiro, Mateus Valadares, Paula Falcão   PR: Gustavo Brasileiro   PC: Laura Barbi
Illustration Artist: Clermont Cintra   CO: Construtora Andrade Gutierrez   AR: Álvaro Hardy (Veveco), Mariza Machado Coelho, Gustavo Penna   P(ss): Jomar Bragança, Rafael Pinho, Cecília Rocha, Mariana Hardy, Fernando Maculan   SB: Mariana Hardy & Fernando Maculan

BRAZIL 2005

CASA DO BAILE   CASSINO   CHURCH SÃO FRANCISCO   YATCH CLUB

MINEIRINHO SPORT ARENA   MINEIRÃO SOCCER STADIUM   SPORTS CLUB   SPORTS CLUB

INFORMATION   PAMPULHA'S AIRPORT   ZOO   FOREST

Pampulha's lake and its surroundings configure an extremely valuable urban area in the city of Belo Horizonte, not only for its privileged landscape but also for its cultural and architectonic character, which was inaugurated with the construction of Oscar Niemeyer's buildings in the 1940's. The signage is part of a recent urban re-qualification project designed by architects Alvaro Hardy, Mariza Machado Coelho and Gustavo Penna, which, with the restoration of Niemeyer's buildings, confirms *de vocation* of Pampulha as a public area.

パンプーラ湖とその周辺地域は美しい景観と歴史ある文化、そして1940年代のオスカー・ニーマイヤー設計による建設に始まる建築的特徴によって、ベロ・オリゾンテ市に極めて貴重な都市区域を形成している。ガイドサインは都市開発計画の一部で、ともにニーマイヤーによる建築物の修復工事とともに、公共スペースとしての役割を確立している。

Pampulha's Ecologic Park

Eco Park エコパーク

CL: Belo Horizonte City Hall
DD: Mariana Hardy & Fernando Maculan   D: Fernando Jorge da Silva, Gustavo Brasileiro, Laura Barbi, Márcio Barbalho
Design Assistants: Alexandre Perocco, Alice Vasconcellos, Ana Bárbara Ivo, André Coelho, Antonio Valladares, Bruno
Teixeira, Carolina Salgado, Cássia Perocco, Cecília Rocha, Danilo Queiroz, Eduardo de Almeida, Gabriela Abdalla,
Joana Carneiro, Mateus Valadares, Paula Falcão   PR: Gustavo Brasileiro   PC: Laura Barbi
Illustration Artist: Clermont Cintra   CO: Construtora Andrade Gutierrez   AR: Álvaro Hardy (Veveco), Mariza
Machado Coelho, Gustavo Penna   P(ss): Jomar Bragança, Rafael Pinho, Cecília Rocha, Mariana Hardy, Fernando
Maculan   SB: Mariana Hardy & Fernando Maculan

BRAZIL 2005

 GYM

 PLAYGROUND

 BANDSTAND

 WATER TREATMENT STATION

 FOUNTAIN

 ENTRANCE

 REST AREA

MAINTENANCE

 ENVIROMENTAL PROTECTION

 BAY

 RUNNIG TRACK

 BIKE RACKS

 PUBLIC CENTER

 SNACK BAR

 WILD AREA

 STAFF DINNING ROOM

 INFORMATION

 ESPLANADE

 FOREST

 HANDICAPED TOILET FACILITIES

 TOILETS, FEMALE

 TOILETS, MALE

 TOILETS, MAN / WOMAN

 KITCHEN

 ADMINISTRATION

 RECEPTION

 MANAGMENT

 AUDITORIUM

 MALE STAFF LOCKER ROOM

 FEMALE STAFF LOCKER ROOM

 RESTRICTED ACCESS

 DANGER

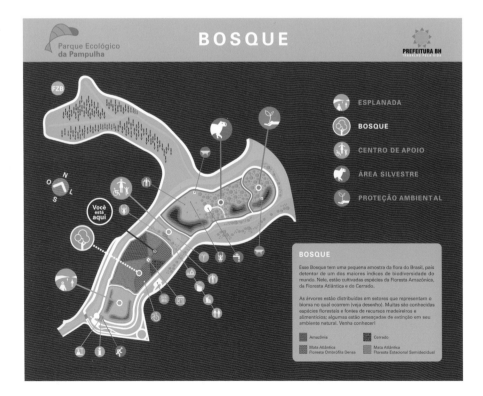

Pampulha's Ecologic Park was designed by Alvaro Hardy, Mariza Machado Coelho and Gustavo Penna as part of the urban area requalification project. The ambient and educational character of this urban equipment encouraged the playful solution in the signage where illustration, together with a variety of materials, forms and colors, made the information more attractive and effective for its visitors.

パンプーラ・エコロジック・パークは都市再開発計画の一部として設計。都市を象徴する雰囲気と教育的特徴は、遊び感覚のソリューションにもとづいて作成。サインにはイラストを用い多様な材質や形と色で訪問者に魅力的で効果的な情報を提供できるよう工夫した。

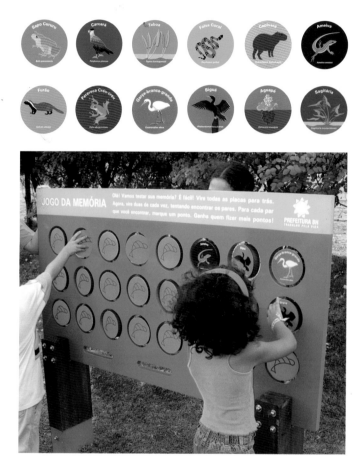

Port of Los Angeles Waterfront Promenade

Waterfront Promenade 遊歩道

CL: Port of Los Angeles
DD: Robin Perkins
D: John Lutz, Erin Carney, Andy Davey, Jose Gavieres, Rick Crane
DF, SB: Selbert Perkins Design
AR: EDAW
P(ss): John Lutz, Andy Davey

USA 2005

The port of Los Angeles Waterfront Promenade features historical and informational interpretive signs, pedestrian, vehicular and bike path signage, and a banner system implemented along the Promenade to promote the new public access areas with icons of local historical monuments.

ロサンゼルス港ウォーターフロント遊歩道には、地域の歴史建造物をかたどったアイコンを採用。新たに一般アクセスができるようになったエリアの促進を目的として、遊歩道沿いに歴史的説明・情報説明サイン、歩行者・自転車道サイン、バナーサインを設置している。

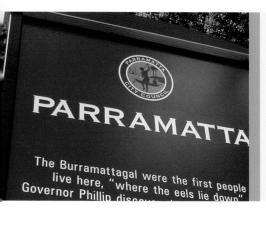

Parramatta City

Public Street　公道

CL: City of Parramatta
PC, DD: Steven Joseph
D: Nicky Hardcastle
DF, P(ss), SB: Spatchurst

AUSTRALIA 2001

The newly developed masterplan for the city's signage encompassed a family of signs for the city entrance, street identity, and directional, location, services and interpretive signage. The criteria driving the design were to establish an identity for the city and to assist visitors and residents in exploring the city further. The masterplan not only established graphic and construction guidelines, but also made budgetary recommendations for its implementation.

市の標識のための新しい全体計画では、市の玄関口・通り・方向・位置・公共機関の案内や説明のためのサインが考案された。デザインにおける一貫した指標は、市のためのVI構築と、訪問者や居住者が市内をより動きやすくすること。また、この全体計画ではグラフィックや建設上の指針だけではなく、予算についての提案も行われた。

Rodrigo de Freitas Lagoon

Lake Park 公園

CL: Bradesco Seguros, Bradesco and BCN
PC: Valéria London
DD: Valéria London, Ana Lucia Velho
D: Atsuhiko Hiratsuka, Luciana Gutierrez, Claudia Gutwilen, Felipe Lobo
P: Marcos Morteira
DF, SB: Valéria London Design

BRAZIL 2001

The Tom Jobim Park, a public section of the Rodrigo de Freitas Lagoon in Rio de Janeiro, ranks among the top scenic spots in the world. The most important criteria in the design development of the environmental signage program for these four big parks were to give clear directional and historical information, have a clean formal treatment and the give the lagoon a distinct graphic approach.

リオ・デ・ジャネイロのロドリゴ・デ・フレイタス湖にある公園、トム・ジョビン・パークは、世界有数の景勝地である。この大きな4つの公園にほどこされた環境サインプログラムでは、方向案内や歴史的な情報を分かりやすく表示すること、すっきり整然としたデザインに仕上げること、この湖の特徴となるような個性的なグラフィックを採用することなどを最重要基準としてデザイン開発が行われた。

São José Farm Golf Club

Golf Club ゴルフクラブ

CL: Conquista
PC, DD, D, AR: Carlos Perrone
P: Eduardo Castantto
DF, SB: Desenhológico
CO: Neo Brasil

BRAZIL 2003

Modular and extremely versatile, this signage system is notable for its efficient synthesis of tradition and innovation using a design pattern typical of Brazilian agricultural regions.

モジュール方式で非常に汎用性の高いこのサインには、ブラジルの農業地域によく見られるデザインパターンが用いられ、伝統と革新とがうまく融合されている。

SESC SP

Leisure & Sports Facilities　レジャー＆スポーツ施設

CL: SESC
S: Álberto Costa
PR: Luiz Eduardo Graziano
PC, DD: André Poppovic
D: Carolina Olsson, Jennifer Abram, Sidney Diniz
DF, SB: Oz Design
CO: 2Rj
P(ss): Carolina Olsson, Eduardo Moraes

BRASIL 2005

An exterior totem and organic forms characterize the individual signage units. The facilities' diffferent activities are represented as pictograms.

外観のトーテムと有機的なフォルムが個々のサインの特徴となっている。この施設内で行われるさまざまなアクティビティがピクトグラム化されている。

Air Canada Center

Sports & Entertainment Facilities　スポーツ施設

CL: Maple Leaf Sports & Entertainment
S, PC, DD: Randy Johnson
P: WSI Signs (Signage)
D: Brenda Tong
P: Kerun IP
DF, SB: Entro Communications
CO: PCL (Building)
AR: Brisbin Brook Beynon Architects

CANADA 1999

Toronto's 20,000 seat hockey and basketball arena, home to NHL's Leafs and the NBA's Raptors. The signage system includes wayfinding and advertising signage. The new arena has been architecturally integrated with the Art Deco and Art Moderne facade. Signage elements, forms, and graphics were developed to reflect architectural features of both styles, and the signage program used materials and finishes to support the image..

2万人収容できるアリーナでNHL「リーフス」とNBA「ラプターズ」の本拠地。サインシステムはウェイファインディング標示と広告標示を含む。競技場の建築様式はアールデコやモダンアート風の外観を採用し、サイン要素や形状、グラフィックはこれらの建築特徴を反映させて作成。サイン計画は競技場のイメージを生かす材料と仕上がり観を意識した。

Brooklyn Cyclones

Stadium スタジアム

PC: Ann Harakawa
DD: Anthony Ferrara
D: Dominic Borgia
SB: Two Twelve Associates

USA 2002

With the creation of the Cyclones (the Mets' Class-A team), baseball has returned to Brooklyn. The signage for the new venue conveys a sense of excitement and love for the game. Inspired by the carnival atmosphere of its Coney Island boardwalk location, the design uses updated colors and an expressive mix of typefaces. Sign types range from wayfinding identifiers and amenities signage, to innovative floor graphics that help fans locate their seats. The signs animate the stadium interior, and a system of exterior banners welcome and inform visitors and fans.

新球場のサインは試合への興奮や愛情が込められ、デザインはコニーアイランドのボードウォーク（遊歩道）に漂うお祭りムードから着想を得た。新たな色彩が用いられ、タイプフェースの組み合わせも表現豊か。サインの種類はウェイファインディング表示、施設を示すサインをはじめ、座席を見つけやすい画期的なフロア表示などがある。こうしたサインによりスタジアムのインテリアに生き生きとした表情が与えられた。

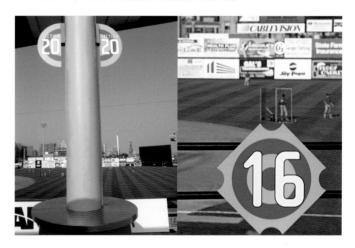

AmericanAirlines Arena

Arena アリーナ

CL: Miami Heat Basketball Properties
S: Jay Cross, President
PR, DD: Stuart Ash
PC: Justin Young
D: Bernhard Muller, Chris Herringer, Michel Schmid, Udo Schliemann
DF, SB: Gottschalk+Ash International
CO: Capital Signs
AR: Arquitectonica

CANADA 2000

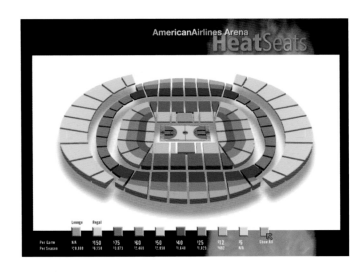

The American Airlines Arena is Miami's hottest sports and entertainment venue. G+A's mandate was to create a branded environment controlling every facet of the visual and graphic expression. As part of the client architecture team, G+A coordinated the continuity of the overall image - from building identification at pedestrian walkways to the themed advertising system, from electronic scoreboards and concessions within the area to the marketing materials used to define a unique, branded environment.

アメリカン航空アリーナのサイン計画はビジュアル、グラフィック表現などのあらゆる面を統制し、環境ブランドを作り上げた。歩道からの建物の識別、テーマごとの広告システム、アリーナ内の電光掲示板や場内売り場、さらにブランド環境を特定するためのマーケティング材料にいたるまで、全般的なイメージを維持することを目指した。

Nissan Stadium　日産スタジアム

Stadium　スタジアム

CL, SB: Nissan Motor, Ltd.　日産自動車
DF: Nissan Motor Co., Ltd. Design Center Global Design Management Design Strategy / Communication
日産自動車デザイン本部グローバルマネジメント部デザイン戦略 / コミュニケーショングループ
CO, AR: Tbwa / Japan Co., Ltd. , Katsura Kogei Co., Ltd., Tanseisha Co., Ltd.　TBWA / Japan　桂工芸　丹青社
P(ss): Akiyoshi Miyashita (New Photo Studio Inc.)　宮下明義（ニューフォトスタジオ）

JAPAN 2005

Nissan Stadium, for which Nissan Motor Co., Ltd. acquired the naming rights in March 2005, has opened. All names around the stadium including transportation facilities and road signs have been upgraded also. LED signage boards and the largest Nissan brand symbols in Japan have been installed in the center of the stadium interior.

2005年3月に、日産自動車がネーミングライツを取得した「日産スタジアム」がオープン。スタジアム周辺の交通機関や道路標識などの名称も全てリニューアルされた。スタジアム内部の中心にはLED仕様のサイン看板と日本最大の日産ブランドシンボルが設置されている。

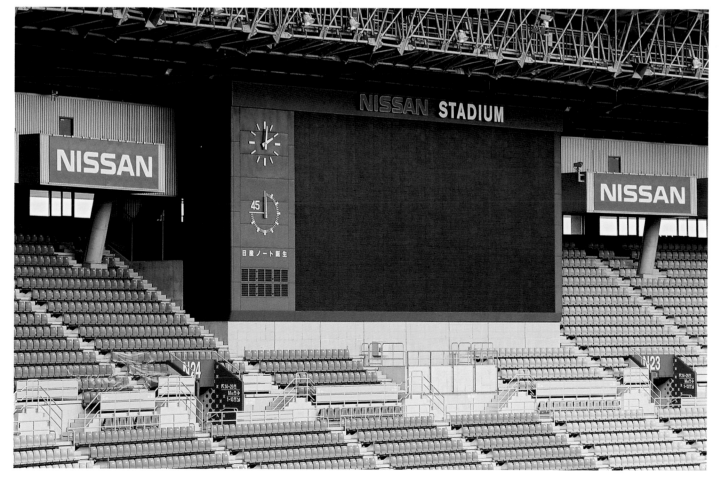

Ivy Stadium　アイビースタジアム

Stadium　スタジアム

CL: Miyazaki City　宮崎市
CO, SB: Kotobuki Corporation　コトブキ
AR: AXS Satow Inc., Nasu Sekkei JV　佐藤総合計画・那須設計共同企業体
P(ss): Shigeru Ohno　大野 繁

JAPAN 2003

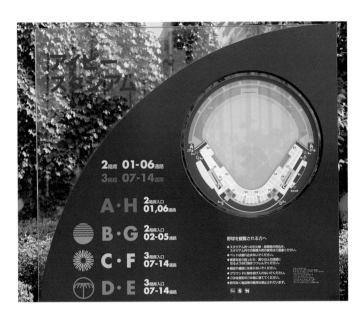

Baseball ground also used as a camp for pro baseball teams, with slopes up to the second tier of seating to accommodate wheelchair access. Vivid colors as intense as the Miyazaki sunlight, such as red, blue and green, were employed for the stadium interior. Each area is color-coded, including seating in the stands, to facilitate visual identification.

プロ野球チームのキャンプ地としても使用されている野球場。車椅子でそのまま上がれるよう2階席までスロープが設けられている。スタジアムは宮崎の太陽の光に負けない赤・青・緑・黄といったビビッドなカラーを採用。エリアごとに色分けをし、スタンドの椅子の色もエリアカラーで揃えることで、視覚的にもより一層わかりやすくなっている。

Kobe Wing Stadium　神戸ウィングスタジアム

Stadium　スタジアム

CL: Kobe City　神戸市
DF: Obayashi Corporation　大林組
CO, SB: Kotobuki Corporation　コトブキ
AR: Obayashi Corporation, Kobe Steel JV　大林組　神戸製鋼JV
P(ss): Tokuaki Takimoto　滝本徳明

JAPAN　2001

© KOBE WING STADIUM

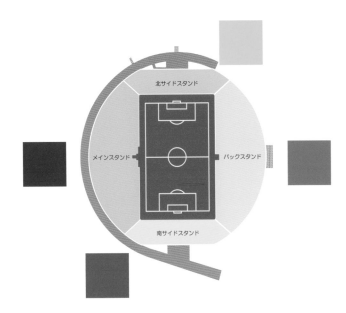

The signage system assigns a different color to each of the 4 stands, creating the image of blocks within the stadium. In addition, the guide sign at the stadium entrance has been created in a 3-dimensional shape of the actual stadium, helping visitors to easily grasp the layout.

サイン計画は、4つのスタンドそれぞれにスタジアムのブロックを意識させるカラーを設定した。また、スタジアムエントランスの案内サインは、実際のスタジアムの形状と同じように板面を立体的に仕上げることで、空間把握を助けている。

※写真は2002年FIFAワールドカップ開催当時。現在、神戸ウイングスタジアムは開閉式の屋根を持つ、全天候型スタジアムです。

American Airline's Center

Arena アリーナ

PC: David Gibson
DD: Anthony Ferrara
D: Alexandra Lee, Dominic Borgia
SB: Two Twelve Associates

USA 2002

Home of the Dallas' NBA basketball and NHL hockey teams, this arena offers a state-of-the-art sports and entertainment experience in a unique, neoclassical building. The wayfinding system offers an elegant, low-key solution that complements the architecture. The signage employed a stylized eagle derived from the AA graphic identity as a unifying decorative motif on key sign types. The planning resulted in a comprehensive information system, ensuring that visitors will not get lost as they navigate the huge and complex building.

ダラスのNBAバスケットボールとNHLホッケーの両チームの本拠地であり、最先端のスポーツ試合やイベントを観戦できる個性的なネオクラシック建築のアリーナに調和したサインは簡素で控えめ。主要デザインパターンには「AA」のシンボルから着想したイーグル模様を使用。広大で複雑な施設内でも観客が迷わないような包括的情報システムが実現。

Amtrak Acela Station

Railroad　鉄道

CL: National Railroad Passenger
D: David Vanden-Eynden, Principal in Charge, Chris Calori, Advisory Principal, Denise Funaro, Jordan Macks
SB: Calori & Vanden-Eynden

USA　(on going)

The objective of the signage program was to create a strong identity for Amtrak's high-speed rail service and introduce across the entire passenger experience: from outside the station, through ticketing and gate areas, to platform. The system was developed as a "kit of parts" to insure uniformity and deploy the various sign units at each station with a minimum of custom fitting. A sensuously curved "airfoil" shape forms the stylistic nucleus of the program, which ranges from large pylons to ceiling- and wall-mounted signs.

アムトラックの高速鉄道サービスの強いイメージの構築と、駅構外から発券窓口および改札を通りプラットホームまでの乗客の誘導を目指したプロジェクト。各駅の様々なサインユニットを「パーツキット」として開発することで工程を均一にし、労力を最小限化。大型案内塔から天井や壁のサインに至るまで、官能的な翼形の曲線がデザインベースとなっている。

Minatomirai Line　みなとみらい線

Railroad　鉄道

CL: Yokohama Minatomirai Railway Company Japan Railway Construction, Transport and Technology Agency
横浜高速鉄道 鉄道建設・運輸整備支援機構 鉄道建設本部 東京支社
DD: Tatsuzo Akase, Toshio Kurokawa (Rei Design & Plannings)　赤瀬達三　黒川敏雄（黎デザイン総合計画研究所）
D: Hirofumi Shinohara, Ayano Kojima (Rei Design & Plannings)　篠原博文　児島あやの（黎デザイン総合計画研究所）
P: Shinichi Tomita　富田眞一
SB: Rei Design & Plannings　黎デザイン総合計画研究所

JAPAN 2004

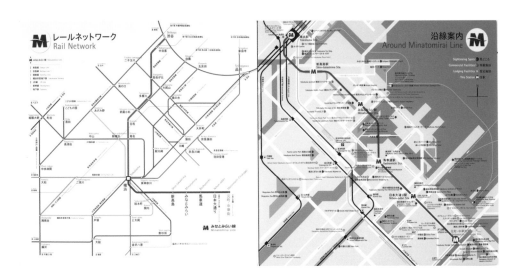

The Minato Mirai subway line began operation in February 2004 connecting Tokyo Shibuya and Yokohama Motomachi. The basic idea was "signage that is legible and intelligible for everyone" and placement of information on the signs, the height at which signs are displayed and typeface selection that meets the needs of users was intensively researched. Effort was also made to create an appropriate image in keeping with the futuristic environment of the rail line.

2004年2月に開業した、東京渋谷と横浜元町を結ぶ地下鉄「みなとみらい線」。サインシステムでは「誰にでも見やすくわかりやすい」を基本理念とし、利用者のニーズを踏まえた情報内容や配置、掲出高さ、フォントの選択などを慎重に検討。先進的な沿線環境にふさわしい路線イメージができるよう、表現にも工夫を重ねた。

Linimo Stations　東部丘陵線駅舎

Railroad　鉄道

CL: Aichi Rapid Transit Co., Ltd.　愛知高速交通
DD, P(ss): Kazuo Tanaka　田中一雄
D: Norihiko Hibiya, Kanji Kato (both: while at GK Sekkei Inc.), Ayako Saito　日比谷憲彦　加藤完治（共に在職時）　斎藤絢子
DF, SB: GK Sekkei Inc.　GK設計　CO: Hyojito Co., Ltd.　表示灯　AR: Nikken Sekkei Ltd.　日建設計
Symbol Mark Design, Color Schemes: Nobuoki Ohtani (Ohtani and Associates) , Shigenobu Ohtani, Akira Shiraki,
Naoki Sato (Aichi Prefectural University of Fine Arts and Music)　大谷伸興（オオタニアンドアソシエイツ）　大谷茂暢
白木 彰　佐藤直樹（愛知県立芸術大学）

JAPAN 2005

Signage for the station building at which linear motor car service was launched for the opening of Expo Aichi 2005. A linear, relaxed and rounded shape, something easy on the eyes, was consciously chosen for signs, while different theme colors and graphic symbols were assigned for each station in an attempt to enhance the unique characteristics of each area and aid travelers in identifying their location.

愛知万博の開催に合わせて開業したリニアモーターカーの駅舎サイン。サイン計画はLinear（線的）で伸びやかな、そして見る人にやさしいラウンドシェイプを意識した。また、全駅に異なるテーマカラーとグラフィックシンボルを設定し、各駅の個性の創出と、識別性の向上を試みた。

Metro

Bus バス

CL, SB: Metro (Los Angeles County Metropolitan Transportation Authority)
DF: Metro Design Studio
P(ss): Deniz Durmus, Neil Sadler

USA 2004

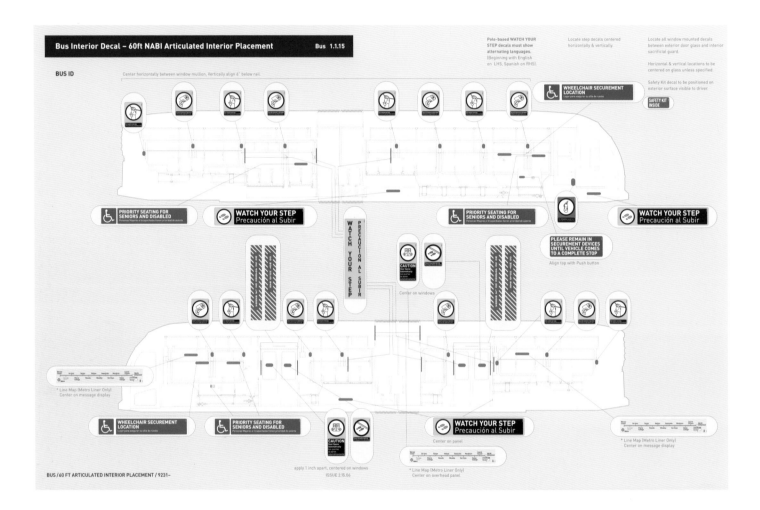

Proprietary Icons designed for Metro let the agency present an authoritative, recognizable yet friendly signage system. Used on 2000 buses and in 73 stations across LA County, the icons add dimension and personality to the instructions displayed. Whether the message is a warning, advice on safety, or just a passenger reminder, the proprietary Metro style always comes through.

Metroバスのサインシステムは信頼性が高く、わかりやすく、親しみやすいアイコンを採用。このアイコンは、ロサンゼルス郡全域を運行する2,000台のバスと73のバス停に貼られている指示書きを新鮮でユニークなものにしている。警告・安全上の注意・乗客への助言等どんなメッセージも、このMetroスタイルでうまく表現されている。

All images are copyright, ©LACMTA and designed by Metro Design Studio

Zürich Airport

Airport　空港

CL: Unique, Flughafen Zürich AG
S: Jörg Rosenberg, Arthur Tobler, Ruedi Stoller
PR: Burri AG and Stoll AG
DD: Ruedi Rüegg
D: Dominik Rinderer, Susanne Tatovski, Ruedi Rüegg
DF, SB: Designalltag Zürich
AR: Nicolas Grimshaw, Itten+Brechbühl, Arge Zayetta

SWITZERLAND 2005

Nr. 1
Flughafen/Airport
nach links

Nr. 1a
Flughafen/Airport
nach rechts

Nr. 2
Ankunft/Arrival
nach links

Nr. 2a
Ankunft/Arrival
nach rechts

Nr. 3
Gates
Abflug/Departure
nach links

Nr. 3a
Gates
Abflug/Departure
nach rechts

Nr. 58
Luftfracht
nach links

Nr. 58a
Luftfracht
nach rechts

Nr. 147
Transfer Desk

Nr. 159
Transfer/
Transfer Gates

Nr. 148
Passkontrolle/
Passport Control,
Immigration

Nr. 149
Ticketkontrolle/
Ticket Control

Nr. 180
Pass- und Ticket-
kontrolle/Passport und
Ticket Control

Nr. 0
Richtungspfeil

Nr. 27/1
Durchgang (Quadrat)

Nr. 27/2
Durchgang (rund)

Nr. 27/3
Richtungspfeil
nach links

Nr. 27/3a
Richtungspfeil
nach rechts

Nr. 27/4
Richtungspfeil wenden
nach links

Nr. 27/4a
Richtungspfeil wenden
nach rechts

Nr. 189
Cushman

Nr. 190
WLAN Hotspot

Nr. 200
Reisemarkt

Nr. 196
Events

Nr. 157
News

Nr. 13
Information/
Service Center

Nr. 18
Geldwechsel/Change

Nr. 19
Telefon

Nr. 104
Billete/Tickets

Nr. 182
Hotelreservationen/
Hotel Reservation

Nr. 17
Kinder/Children

Nr. 127
Spielzimmer/
Playground

Signaletics means sending signals: signals that indicate the way from points A to B for people unfamiliar with the surroundings. These wayfinders consist of words, pictograms, and arrows. Signaletics also delivers information: destinations (passport control, gates), flight information (arrivals, departures), and the locations of service providers (shopping). One of the important missions of signaletics is to address the needs of all users of the facility, included the visually impaired.

Signaleticsの意味は周辺地域に不案内な人にA地点からB地点への方向を示す信号を送ること。目的地情報（入国審査、搭乗口など）、航空機運航情報（到着便、出発便情報）、ショッピング街の位置情報などのウェイファインディングも言語、絵文字、および矢印で構成している。視覚障害者を含めたすべての空港施設利用者のニーズに対応する点を重視した。

Guangzhou International Airport (Guangzhou City, China)
広州白雲国際空港（中国・広東省広州市）

Airport　空港

CL: Baiyun International Airport Co., Ltd.　広州白雲国際空港
DD: Isao Miyazawa (GK Sekkei Inc.)　宮沢功（GK設計）
D: Norihiko Hibiya (while at GK Sekkei Inc.), Taro Watanabe (Emotional Space Design Inc.)
日比谷憲彦（GK設計／在職時）　渡辺太郎（エモーショナル・スペース・デザイン）
DF, SB: GK Sekkei Inc.　GK設計

CHINA 2004

Signage design was developed to blend in with the materials used in the columns and suspensions, creating an image of the informational display floating in the atmosphere like a cloud. In handling the rather unique spatial structure of three continuous wings - Terminal, Connector, and Concourse - the signs were used to make the change into a new area obvious at each junction. In addition, integrating airport maps in the PDP displays at the information centers unified flight information.

サインデザインは支柱や吊り材を極力空間に溶け込ませるなど工夫し、標示のみが「白雲」のように中空に浮遊するさまをイメージ。ターミナル、コネクト、コンコースという3棟が連なる複雑な空間特性を踏まえ、各結節点をサインによって顕在化した。また、案内拠点には空港内の案内図とPDP表示することでフライトインフォメーションの一体化を図った。

Ottawa Macdonald-Cartier International Airport

Airport　空港

CL: Ottawa Macdonald-Cartier Int'l Airport Authority
S: David Caulfield, VP Airport Development
PR: Stuart Ash
PC, DD: Chris Herringer
D: Udo Schliemann, Chris Herringer, Terry Heard
DF, SB: Gottschalk+Ash International
CO: Taylor Manufacturing
AR: YOW Consultants-a joint venture of Architectura, Brisbin Brook Beynon & Arup

CANADA 2003

Ottawa International Airport underwent a major redevelopment with the design of a new 26 gate passenger terminal. G+A provided a bold, highly visible post-mounted sign system which supports a clear hierarchy of primary and secondary information and electronic signage. G+A won the 2004 Gold Award for wayfinding master planning and implementation from the Society of Environmental Graphic Designers.

オタワ国際空港の大規模な再開発事業で26ゲート付の新旅客ターミナルが設計されるにあたりGottschalk + Ash Internationalは一次・二次情報の優先順位を明確にしたうえ電子サインもサポートした、大胆で非常に目立つポール取り付け式サインシステムを提供。経路案内の総合計画・導入に対し、環境グラフィック・デザイナー協会より2004年度金賞を授与された。

中部国際空港提供

Central Japan International Airport Passenger Terminal Building　中部国際空港旅客ターミナルビル

Airport　空港

CL: Central Japan International Airport Co., Ltd.　中部国際空港
DD: Hiroyuki Akashi (Nikken Sekkei Ltd.)　赤司博之（日建設計）
D, P(ss): Keiichi Koyama (i Design)　児山啓一（アイ・デザイン）　DF: i Design Inc.　アイ・デザイン
CO: Tansei-Sha, Aisei-Sya　丹青社　アイセイ社　AR: Nikken, Azusa, HOK, Arup Central Japan International Airport
Design Consortium　日建・梓・HOK・アラップ中部国際空港旅客ターミナルビル設計監理共同企業体
SB: Nikken Sekkei Ltd.　日建設計

JAPAN　2005

案内所　情報コーナー　お手洗　男性　女性　身障者用設備　乳幼児用設備　オストメイト対応設備　ファミリートイレ　水飲み場

チェックイン／受付　忘れ物取扱所　ホテル／宿泊施設　救護所　警察　休憩所／待合室　特別室　ミーティングポイント　電話　ファックス

銀行・両替　キャッシュサービス　郵便　手荷物一時預かり所　コインロッカー　カート　エレベーター　エスカレーター　階段　喫煙所

クローク　更衣室　更衣室（女子）　シャワー　温泉　展望デッキ　きっぷうりば／精算所　自動販売機　くず入れ　湯沸室

航空機／空港　出発　到着　乗り継ぎ　手荷物受取所　鉄道／鉄道駅　船舶／フェリー／港　バス／バスのりば　タクシー／タクシーのりば　レンタカー

駐車場　税関／荷物検査　出国手続／入国手続／検疫／書類審査　酒類　たばこ　香水　動物検疫　動物検疫　植物検疫　植物検疫

レストラン　喫茶・軽食　バー　店舗／売店　複合施設（スカイタウン）　会計　新聞・雑誌　薬局　理容／美容　手荷物宅配

出　発　Departures
旅客用出発系

到　着　Arrivals
旅客用到着系

電　話　Telephones
旅客用施設系

国제선 출발　国際線出発　International Departures　国際線
国내선 출발　国内航線出発　Domestic Departures　国内線

国際線バナー　国内線バナー

Central Japan International Airport was the first airport in Japan to incorporate the concept of "universal design" comprehensively from the design stage. Intelligibility and visibility where considerations in the development of the visual signage, which has been designed to convey important elements of information based on the concept of "intuitively intelligible signage" in keeping with the aims of universal design.

中部国際空港は、設計の段階からユニバーサルデザインを本格的に導入した日本初の空港。情報伝達の重要な要素を占めるビジュアルサインは、わかりやすさ、見やすさへの配慮、ユニバーサルデザインを達成するために「直感的によくわかるサイン」をコンセプトに設計。乗り継ぎの利便性や段差のない移動など、空港全体がストレスフリーの空間を演出している。

Calgary International Airport

Airport 空港

CL: Calgary International Airport Authority
S: Bruce McFarlane, Director of Airport Development
PR: Stuart Ash   PC, DD: Chris Herringer
D: Terry Heard, Katalin Kovats, Doreen Colonello, Jonathan Picklyk, Jamie Cheung, Kal Jabusch
P, P(ss): Rik Kokotovich   DF, SB: Gottschalk+Ash International
CO: Taylor Manufacturing
AR: Cohos Evamy and NBBJ Architects

CANADA 2005

The introduction of the new wayfinding system at the Calgary International Airport provides for enhanced levels of service to the public. A bold, highly visible sign system supports a clear hierarchy of primary and secondary bilingual information. The program includes wayfinding for the 95,000 square meter passenger terminal, rental car center, roadways, parking and curbside areas.

カルガリー国際空港では新経路案内システムを導入したことで利用客へのサービスが向上。視認性の高い、はっきりとしたサインシステムが、二カ国語の一次・二次情報の優先順位を明確に示している。このプロジェクトでは9万5千平方メートルにおよぶ旅客ターミナル、レンタカーセンター、道路、駐車場、縁石等のための経路案内が制作された。

LAX Gateway

Airport　空港

CL: Los Angeles International Airport
DD: Robin Perkins, Clifford Selbert
D: Nick Groh, Clint Woesner
DF, SB: Selbert Perkins Design
AR: Various
P(ss): Anton Grassl

USA　2000-2004

The dramatic gateway into Los Angeles International Airport includes 32-foot high LAX letter forms, a ring of fifteen 120-foot pylons forming a bold gateway into LAX, as well as equally-spaced columns that steadily increase in height along a two-mile roadway median leading up to the gateway. This gateway ring design was symbolic of the "City of Angeles," with the multiple colors representing the multi-cultural city, one of the most diverse in the nation.

ロサンゼルス国際空港の壮大なゲートウェイには、高さ32フィート（9.754m）のLAXの文字が配され、リング状に並べられた120フィート（36.576m）のパイロン15本が堂々たるゲートウェイを演出している。また、入り口まで約3.2km続く道路の中央には、徐々に高くなっていく柱が等間隔に配置されている。このゲートウェイのリング状のデザインは、「シティ・オブ・エンジェル」ことロサンゼルスを象徴するもので、複数の色が使われているが、これはこの街がアメリカでも特に多様性に富んだ多文化都市であることを表現している。

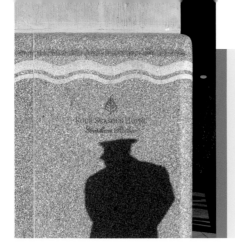

Four Seasons Gresham Palace

Hotel ホテル

CL: Four Seasons Hotel Group
DD: David Hillman
D: David Hillman, Deborah Osborne
DF: Pentagram
SB: Pentagram Design Ltd.

Hungary 2004

The renaissance of an Art Nouveau landmark, exquisitely transformed with ultramodern comforts, this Four Seasons hotel combines intuitive service with panoramic vistas of the Danube and the hills of Buda. The visual identity program includes everything from brochures, menus and room amenities to a comprehensive signage program. The designers have employed a palette in thrall to the building's beautiful Art Nouveau detailing, with floral decorative elements and period typography throughout, using high quality materials and production standards.

アールヌーボー・ルネッサンスの歴史建築がモダンで快適なホテルに。ダニューブ川とブダの丘のパノラマ景観と直感的サービスが融合したホテルのVIプロジェクトは、パンフレット・メニュー・アメニティ・サインシステムを網羅。アールヌーボー建築の細部にあわせて花の装飾や歴史的フォントが使われ、良質な素材使いと高いデザイン基準が保たれた。

Okura Chiba Hotel　オークラ千葉ホテル

Hotel　ホテル

CL: Chiba Municipalities Employees Benefit Association　千葉県市町村職員共済組合
DD: Ryo T. Urano　リョウ T. ウラノ
D: Toshio Takeda　竹田紀雄
DF, SB: Takeda Communication Inc.　ティーシーアイ
CO: Keisei Store, Keisei Department Store　京成ストア　京成百貨店
AR: Nikken Sekkei, Nikken Space Design　日建設計　日建スペースデザイン

JAPAN 2001

Upgrade of the Chiba City, Town and Village Employees Mutual Aid Building to a hotel to be operated by the Okura Hotel. The logo and "subpattern" have been developed with a consciousness of Chiba's vibrant image with a motif of rape blossoms and butterflies. The design incorporates tradition and form, complementing the artworks which are part of the interior design.

千葉県市町村職員共済会館が、オークラホテルの運営するホテルにリニューアル。菜の花と蝶をモチーフにした、千葉の明るいイメージを意識してマークとサブパターンを開発。インテリアにアイアンワークが存在するホテルにマッチした、伝統と格式のあるデザイン。

Hotel Monterey Edelhof ホテルモントレ エーデルホフ札幌

Hotel　ホテル

CL: Maruito Corporation　マルイト
D, AR, SB: Kajima Design　KAJIMA DESIGN
P(ss): Nacása & Partners Inc.　ナカサアンドパートナーズ

JAPAN 2000

The design for the Hotel Montery Group, which has 13 hotels throughout the country, uses a different theme for each hotel, the motif being a historical European city. The design concept of the Edelhof Sapporo is "Vienna at the end of the 19th century, emitting a fascinating light of the revolutionary period." The concept has been consistently applied from the building exterior to the interior design, furniture, artwork and the details in the signage.

全国に13軒を構えるホテルモントレシリーズは、西洋の歴史的な都市をモチーフに、各ホテルで異なるテーマのデザインが展開されている。エーデルホフ札幌のデザインコンセプトは「時代の変革期として魅力的な光を放つ19世紀末のウイーン」。建物外観からインテリア、家具、アートワークそしてサインの細部に至るまで一貫してコンセプトに沿って追求されている。

Hotel the b'

Hotel　ホテル

CL: Ishin Hotels Group Co., Ltd.　イシン・ホテルズ・グループ
PC: W Design International　W Design International Y K.
DF (Logo): Beacon Communications k.k.　ビーコンコミュニケーションズ
DD, D, DF, CO, SB: T.Glover Co., Ltd.　テイ・グラバー

JAPAN 2004

The first letter of each of the concept words "balance" "basic" and "beauty" was used in the naming of the hotel. The aim of the signage design was a modern form and simple structure with the design of the logo emphasizing the letter "b" as a key letter.

ホテルのネーミングは、コンセプトワードの「balance」「basic」「beauty」の頭文字を用いている。サインデザインは、キーワードとなるアルファベット「b」にポイントを置いて作成されたロゴマークのデザインをモチーフに、モダンな形状、シンプルな構成を心掛けた。

OU Land / OU Hotel　おーゆ・ランド　おーゆ・ホテル

Hot Spring Facility　温浴施設

CL: Kaike Onsen Kankou　皆生温泉観光
PR: Ataru Tsuchiya　土屋 中
DD, Total Design Producer: Kohzo Okada　岡田宏三
DF: OD Corporation　オーディ
CO, SB: Kotobuki Corporation　コトブキ
AR: Nikken Sekkei　日建設計
AR, P(ss): Nikken Space Design　日建スペースデザイン
P(ss): Tokuaki Takimoto　滝本徳明

JAPAN 2004

The newly constructed hotel and public hot spring facility is part of the Kaike Onsen Kankou 80th anniversary celebration; enhancing enjoyment of life in the 21st century. The unique name "OU Land" comes from the two magnificent baths - one shaped as an "O" and one shaped as a "U"; "o-u" also means "hot water" in Japanese. Transfiguring this concept into a simple yet impressive graphic design for ads and signs has shown highly successful results for advertising campaigns.

21世紀に向けて、皆生温泉観光80周年に合わせ建設されたホテル併設の民間温浴施設。天然木の風合いを活かしたシンプルな本体設計に、丸いO形湯舟の大浴場「おー風呂」と、珍しいU形湯舟の大浴場「ゆー風呂」を設営することで「OUランド」というネーミングが誕生。そのコンセプトを、シンプルでインパクトのあるグラフィック表現を用いて広告やサインに展開した結果、大きな宣伝効果をもたらした。

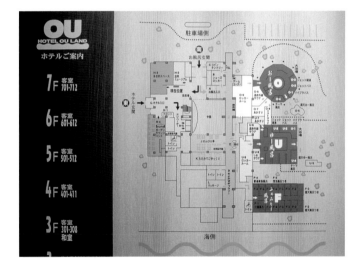

Bungo Oyama Hibiki no Sato　豊後・大山　ひびきの郷

Leisure Facilities　レジャー施設

CL: Zenhachiro Mitoma　三苫善八郎（大分県日田郡大山町町長）
PR, PC: Akira Sanada　真田 彬（P & P）
DD: Motoo Nakanishi　中西元男（中西元男事務所《Paos》）
D: Akihiko Kimura, Miyuki Kameya (both: Enviro-System Inc.)　木村明彦　亀谷美幸（共にエンバイロ・システム）
DF: Norito Shinmura　新村則人（新村デザイン事務所）
SB: Enviro-System Inc.　エンバイロ・システム

JAPAN 2003

リキュール工房
うしゅく

体験工房
こころみ

梅の香温泉
なごりの湯

ふるさと料理
ひびき

お宿
あさもや

Signage plan for work on Hibiki no Sato, a tourist center in the town of Oyama, home of the original "One Village One Product" initiative. A community identity strategy was introduced, and guidelines compiled setting out the design criteria. The project encompassed all aspects of signage design from information signs featuring some of the delightful plants and animals found in Oyama's lovely natural surroundings, to special products from the region.

一村一品運動の元祖、大山町の観光拠点となる「ひびきの郷」整備によるサイン計画。コミュニティ・アイデンティティ戦略を導入し、デザインの基準を示すガイドラインを作成した。大山町の豊かな自然に生息する愛らしい動植物をモチーフに、案内サインから特産品にいたるまで、トータルなデザインを展開した。

Blue Tree Park Hotel - Angra dos Reis

Resort Hotel リゾートホテル

CL: Chieko Aoki Management Company
Project: Blue Tree Park Hotel / Angra dos Reis
PC: Valéria London
DD: Valéria London, Ana Lúcia Velho
D: Atsuhiko Hiratsuka, Luciana Gutiérrez, Claudia Gutwilen
P: Marcos Morteira
DF, SB: Valéria London Design

BRAZIL 2000

The famous Brazilian modernist painter Tarsila do Amaral was chosen to introduce the guests of Blue Tree Park Hotel in Angra dos Reis to some important aspects of Brazilian art. The entire set of items designed, from graphics to signage, are linked through strong images, and formal coherence and unity, while assigning them functional uses in the context of the different areas of the hotel, assuring them comfortable surroundings.

アングラ・ドス・ヘイスにあるブルーツリーパーク・ホテルではブラジル美術の真髄を宿泊客に伝えようとブラジルの著名な現代美術画家タルシラ・ド・アマラルをデザインに起用。グラフィックスからサインまで全アイテムが強いイメージとフォーマルな統一感で結ばれるようデザインされ、ホテルの様々なエリアを機能的に演出。心地よい環境を提供した。

Gaylord Texan Resort & Convention Center

Resort Hotel ホテル

CL: Gaylord Entertainment
Fabricator: AGI (Virginia Beach, VA)
PC: Chung Youl Yoo
DD: Jan Lorenc
D: Jan Lorenc, Chung Youl Yoo
DF, SB: Lorenc+Yoo Design
P(ss): Jan Lorenc, Jisun An

USA 2004

A large resort hotel on the outskirts of Dallas with an overall Old West theme. The sign package features almost 100 different sign types.

ダラス郊外にある全体にウェスタンをテーマにしたホテル。サインシステムでは約100種類のサインを使っている。

Morongo Casino, Resort and Spa

Resort Facilities リゾート施設

CL: Morongo Band of Mission Indians
DD: Robin Perkins
D: John Lutz, Andy Davey, Jose Gavieres, Erin Carney, Georgia Robrecht
DF, SB: Selbert Perkins Design
AR: Jerde Partnership
P(ss): Doug Park

USA 2004

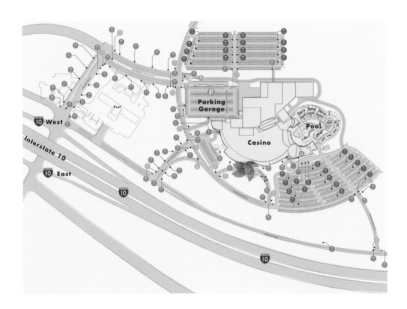

The master plan for the environmental graphics for the hotel, casino and spa encompassed identity pylon sign, pedestrian and vehicular wayfinding systems and interactive hotel directory kiosks. The scope work extended to naming and logos for the spa, restaurants and bars, and design of the different menus, business stationery, hotel amenities and uniforms for the entire hotel and casino.

パイロンサイン、歩行者・車両用経路案内システム、双方向のホテル案内端末が考案された、ホテル・カジノ・スパ向け環境グラフィックスの基本計画。このプロジェクトでは、スパ・レストラン・バーのロゴ、様々なメニュー、ステーショナリー、アメニティ、ホテル・カジノ用のユニフォームも制作された。

Nacional Supermarket

Supermarket スーパーマーケット

CL: Sonae
S: Roberto Bastos
PR: Carlos Maltez
PC: Márcio Lopes
DD: Leonardo Araújo
D: Gabriel Gallina, Alessandra Pollo
DF, SB: Gad'design
CO: Megapainéis, Estampa, Imprima

BRAZIL 2005

The project aimed at realizing the concept defined for the Nacional Supermercados brand: "Alma de Almac" (grocery shop soul). The entire visual communication system and the store setting defined a new standard for the premiere store of Porto Alegre's first 24-hour supermarket.

ナシオナル・スーパーマーケットのブランド・コンセプトAlma de Almac (食料品店の心意気) を形にするためのプロジェクト。総合的な視覚コミュケーションシステムと店舗展開が、ポルト・アレグレ初の24時間営業高級スーパーマーケットの新しいスタンダードを生んだ。

Peruzzo Supermarket

Supermarket スーパーマーケット

CL: Peruzzo
S: Roberto Bastos
PR: André Renard
PC: Gabriel Gallina
DD: Leonardo Araújo
D: Alessandra Pollo, André Marsiglia
DF, SB: Gad'design
CO: LKG

BRAZIL 2005

The signage system project aimed at valorizing and reinforcing the Peruzzo brand identity through an easy-to-read informative language, differentiation of settings, and a low execution cost.

情報をすぐに理解できるわかりやすい言語表現、各設定の差別化、実施コストの抑制を実現することで、安定した価格設定とPeruzzoのブランド・アイデンティティ強化を目指したサインシステム計画。

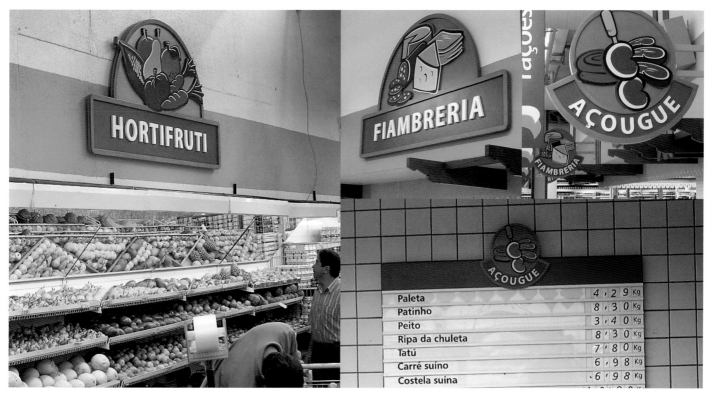

World Trade Center

Commercial Complex　複合商業施設

CL, PR: World Trade Center
DD, D, P, P(ss): Sudarshan Dheer
DF, SB: Graphic Communication Concepts
AR: Firoz Kurianwala

INDIA 2002

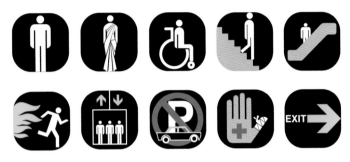

The Shopping Arcade is a part of the World Trade Center complex. It comprises two floors each with two distinct sections, each of which is color-coded. A three-dimensional map at the entrance identifies the zones. Color-coding runs onto the ceiling to indicate the area in which one is standing. At every junction there is a map to indicate the shops to the left and right.

このワールド・トレード・センターにはショッピングアーケードが併設。2階建てのビルの各フロアが2セクションに分かれ、サインシステムによって全セクションが色分けされた。エントランスの立体地図は各ゾーンを案内。歩行者は天井に表示された色を見れば自分の所在地を把握できる。交差点ごとにおかれた地図は左右に並ぶショップをガイド。

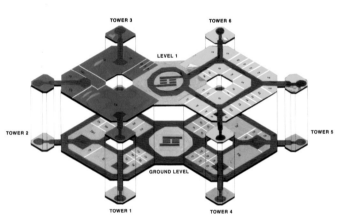

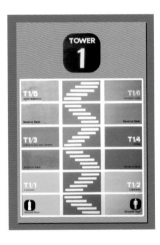

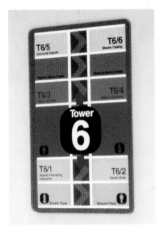

Polaris Fashion Place

Commercial Complex 複合商業施設

CL: Glimcher Development Company
S, PR, AR: KA, Inc. Architecture
PC: David Park
DD: Jan Lorenc
D: Jan Lorenc, Chung Youl Yoo, David Park
DF, SB: Lorenc+Yoo Design
AR: Landscape Architecture; KA. Inc. Architecture
P(ss): Polaris Fashion Place

USA 2000

Polaris Fashion Place is a two-story enclosed regional mall with seven anchors, over 400,000 square feet of leasable mall shop area and a food court. The mall's theme is that of a country club or the concierge area of a grand hotel. Volume spaces were made more intimate than those found in many regional malls, to allow for better use of budgeted dollars on upgraded finishes, moldings and furnishings than would have been possible in a larger space.

ポラリス・ファッション・プレイスは7つの建物からなる2階建てのモール。テナントエリアとフードコートを併せた広さは3万7千平方メートル以上に及ぶ。そのテーマはカントリークラブやホテルのコンシェルジェに近く、多くの大型モールとは異なり広い空間に心地よいムードが漂う。今までのモールにはなかった高級な装具や調度品に囲まれ、有意義な買物が楽しめる。

The Lodge at Bellevue Square

Commercial Complex 複合商業施設

CL: Kemper Development Co.
DD: Michael Courtney
D: Michael Courthey, Jennifer Comer, Heidi Favour
DF, SB: Michael Courthey Design, Inc.
P(ss): Tom McMackm

USA 2001

The Lodge is the centerpiece of a multimillion-dollar expansion to Bellevue Square – the premier shopping destination in the Pacific Northwest, attracting over 16 million visitors each year. The comprehensive, environmental graphics program builds upon the architectural concept of an upscale, northwestern retreat and features natural materials such as structural timbers, etched copper, and river rocks. Program elements include exterior signage, custom directories, and several styles of wayfinding trail markers.

ザ・ロッジは毎年1600万人の観光客が訪れるベルヴ・スクエアに拡張したショッピング・モール。総合環境グラフィックは北西部の静養地を建築コンセプトに、プログラム要素に屋外表示、カスタムディレクトリ、ウェイファインディング・トレイル・マーカーを採用。構造木材やエッチング処理を施した銅、河川にある岩石などの自然素材を使用している。

World Market Center

Convention Center コンベンションセンター

CL: World Market Center
DD: Robin Perkins
D: John Lutz, Andy Davey, Kevin Stevens, Erin Carney
DF, SB: Selbert Perkins Design
AR: Jerde Partnership
P(ss): Andy Davey

USA 2005

Identity and wayfinding system for the World Market Center, a hospitality contract furnishings showroom and convention complex in Las Vegas. Ten-foot-high freestanding letters identify the Center for arriving visitors, while a 39-foot tall illuminated identity tower and corresponding building ID identify the landmark building from afar. A crisp, modern wayfinding system helps visitors navigate the 12 million square foot complex.

応接家具のショールームとコンベンション施設が併設されたラスベガスのワールド・マーケットセンターのサイン・案内システム。建物正面の高さ約3mの文字が並ぶ施設名のデザインは訪問客がセンターを識別しやすくしたもの。地上約12mの位置にあるセンターのサイン付電飾塔により、建物を遠くからでも確認できる。モダンな道案内システムは約111万平方メートルの施設を明瞭にガイド。

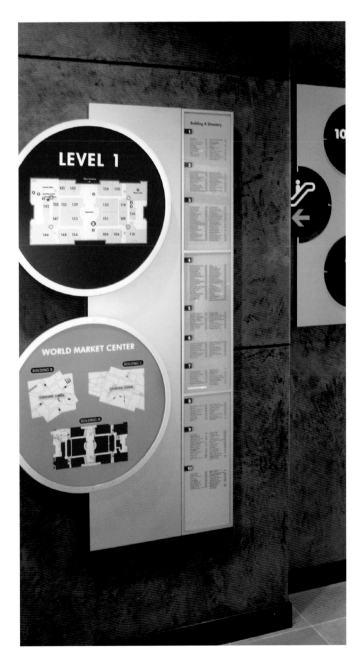

The Bond

Office Building　オフィスビル

CL, PC: Bovis Lend Lease (BLL)
PC: BLL
DD: Carlo Giannasca
D: Carlo Giannasca, Kasia Wydrowski, Joanna Mackenzie, Bridget Atkinson
DF, SB: Frost Design, Sydney
CO: Atree Signs
AR: BLL / Peddle Thorp Walker
P(ss): Kraig Carlstrom

AUSTRALIA 2005

Our brief was to provide signage that complemented the building's stance as ecologically sound architecture of the future and reflected the site's rich history and natural surroundings. Names and graphics metaphorically represent the layered history of the site. Clear messaging and unobtrusive forms of the signage reflect the clean line of the architecture. The earthy primary sign colors reflect the natural environment/stone and the use of etched linear elements of varying thickness pay homage to the exposed layers in the rock.

この建物がテーマとする「生態系に調和した未来建築」の補完と、周辺の豊かな歴史・自然の反映を目指したサインデザイン。名前とグラフィックは周囲で重ねられてきた歴史の隠喩。サインが持つ明解なメッセージと控えめなデザインは建築の方針を反映したもの。素朴な色あいは自然環境や石を表し、様々な太さの線のエッチングは岩石に表出した地層へのオマージュ。

Homemaker City

Commercial Complex　複合商業施設

CL: Property Solutions Group
PC: Jack Bryce-Principal
D: John Ellway-Senior Designer
DF, SB: Minale Bryce Design Strategy
CO: Kiss Graphics
AR: Woods Bagot
P(ss): David Sandison

AUSTRALIA　2005

The primary aim was to maximize tenants' branding space and integrate the signage into the architecture. The program covered large pylon signage, Centre furniture, parking and pedestrian directional signage and public-art environmental graphics. Many of the signage elements take on a stacked "cube" design, a reference to packaging boxes relating to the building's function as a bulky goods retail centre. The color palette is derived from the exterior architecture and uses a simple combination of orange, gray, silver, black and white.

テナントのブランディング効果の最大化と、建築とサインの融合を目指したプロジェクト。大型パイロンサイン、中央の什器、駐車場・歩行者用の標識、公共空間用のグラフィック等が制作された。箱を積み重ねたサインの形は巨大なショッピングセンターの包装箱をイメージ。色彩は建物外観を基調にオレンジ、灰、銀、黒、白がシンプルに組みあわされた。

North Market Building

Commercial Complex 複合商業施設

CL: A.F. Gilmore Company
S: Julie Kleinick
PC, D: Carol Newsom, Lucy Gonzalez
DD: Carol Newsom
DF, SB: Newsom Design
AR: Koning Eizenberg Architecture
P(ss): Angelica Solis

USA 2004

The project brief was to design a building identity that would follow the architectural cues and be seen as separate from, but not overpower, the ground floor tenant signage. The scope included exterior building and garage signage, lobby directories, tenant office plaques, and an exterior monument sign. The building's materials provided the inspiration for the sign program materials: satin finish aluminum, colored glass panels, and a bold color palette.

プロジェクトの目標は、建築にマッチしつつも差別化され、しかも1階のテナント用サインを霞ませることのないサインデザイン。建物の外装・駐車場用サイン、ロビーの案内板、テナント用サイン、屋外のモニュメントサインなどが制作された。建物の素材にあわせて、サインには、つや消し仕上アルミ、色ガラスパネル、鮮やかな色彩が採用された。

JR Central Towers　JRセントラルタワーズ

Commercial Complex　複合商業施設

CL: Central Japan Railway Company　東海旅客鉄道
PC: Akitoshi Furukawa　古川彰俊
DD: Gaku Ohta　太田 岳
D: Gaku Ohta, Osamu Kuwata　太田 岳　桑田 修
DF, SB: Nippon Design Center　日本デザインセンター

JAPAN 1999

Multi-purpose commercial structure towering above JR Nagoya Station. Recognized by Guinness Book of World Records as the world's tallest station building, JR Central Towers has a base of 18 lower-level floors, topped by the 200m high-rise twin towers. The entire structure consists of the office tower and the 53-story hotel tower. The anchor department store occupies two underground floors and 11 above-ground floors. Nagoya's new landmark exudes vital information and ideas with refreshing charm and allure.

JR名古屋駅上にそびえ立つ総合複合ビル。18階建ての低層部とその上の200m超級のツインタワーからなり、世界一高い駅ビルとしてギネスブックに認定された。建物はオフィス棟と53階建てのホテル棟からなり、地下2階から地上11階までをデパートが占める。名古屋のランドマークとして新鮮で魅力あふれる情報を発信している。

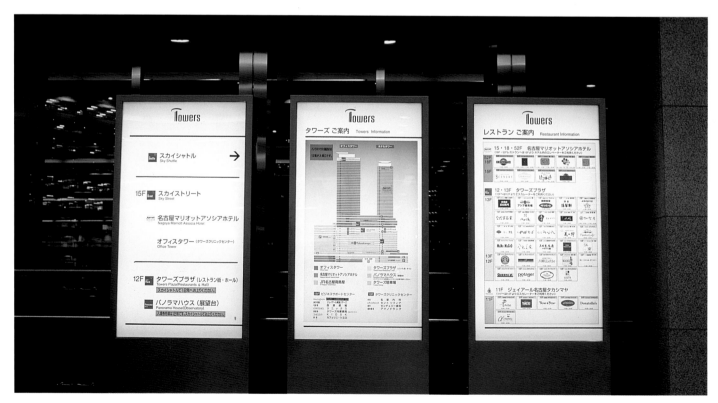

Ecute Ōmiya　エキュート大宮

Commercial Complex　複合商業施設

CL: JR East Station Retailing Co., Ltd.　JR東日本ステーションリテーリング
DD: Gaku Ohta　太田 岳
D: Gaku Ohta, Toshihiko Morita　太田 岳　森田利彦
DF, SB: Nippon Design Center　日本デザインセンター

P(ss): Ryo Tanaka　田中 亮

JAPAN　2005

Signage for the 69-store commercial concourse located inside the ticket barriers at the South entrance of Omiya Station. The signs express the fun and lively atmosphere of a space that brings people of all sorts together. Creating a charming excursion mood in the area while clearly transferring of important information, the signs promote products and services of high quality and orininginality. The result is an area of fun, featuring flexibility and entertaining variations.

69店舗が店を構える大宮駅南口改札内のエキナカ商業空間。あらゆる人が集う「にぎわい」や「楽しさ」を表現しているecuteサイン。街の回遊性を演出する環境空間の創出、地域情報発信機能の充実を図り、高品質でオリジナリティーあふれる商品とサービスを提供。フレキシブルでバリエーション豊かな空間を創造している。

Akasaka Inter City　赤坂インターシティ

Commercial Complex　複合商業施設

CL: Kowa Real Estate Co., Ltd.　興和不動産
S, AR: Nihon Sekkei, Inc.　日本設計
DD, P(ss): Keizo Ochi (T.Glover Co., Ltd.)　越智啓三（テイ・グラバー）
D: Mami Yamamoto (T.Glover Co., Ltd.)　山本麻実（テイ・グラバー）
DF, CO, SB: T.Glover Co., Ltd.　テイ・グラバー

JAPAN 2005

Signage of a high quality using a linear motif that harmonizes the design with the architectural exterior of the office/apartment complex. The aim was to minimize the "eyesore" effect for workers and residents by making the visitor signage as small as practical, to blend in with the environment and enhance the quality of the space.

生活者の視点を重視した住居とオフィスであるため、来訪者へのサインは必要最小限とし、高いクオリティーのサインデザインを目指した。建築外装と調和する「線」をデザインエレメントとすることで、環境と調和しながら、その空間の質を高めるようなサインデザインが実現した。

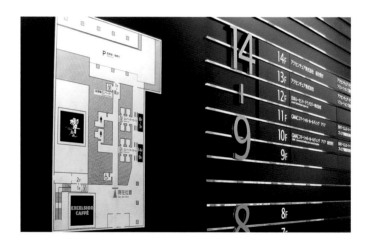

Shinagawa Seaside East&West Tower
品川シーサイドイースト・ウエストタワー

Commercial Complex　複合商業施設

CL: SST. East Spc, SST. West Spc, Mitsubishi Trust and Banking Co., Ltd.
SSTイースト特定目的会社　SSTウエスト特定目的会社　三菱信託銀行
PC: Jones Lang LaSalle Co., Ltd.　ジョーンズ ラング ラサール
DD: Tetsuichi Tomonaga (T.Glover Co., Ltd.)　朝永徹一（テイ・グラバー）
D: Yuki Ide (T.Glover Co., Ltd.)　井出由紀（テイ・グラバー）
DF, CO, SB: T.Glover Co., Ltd.　テイ・グラバー　P(ss): Susumu Koshimizu　輿水 進
JAPAN　2005

Recently we have seen a forest of colorless large-scale redevelopments pop up. Realizing the importance of creating a building's identity, we have come up with a sign program using the official name of the building as the logo mark, transforming it into symbols, and applying other methods in an attempt to enhance the level of appeal to the user.

近年、大規模な再開発地域内で無個性化したビルが林立している。そうした状況の中、今回のサイン計画では、ビルの固有名称をロゴマークとして構築、記号化させるなど、利用者への訴求力向上を目指し、ビルディングアイデンティティの顕在化を計ることが必要と考えた。

Muza Kawasaki, Muza Kawasaki Symphony Hall
ミューザ川崎　ミューザ川崎シンフォニーホール

Commercial Complex　複合商業施設

CL, AR: U.D.C　都市基盤整備公団 神奈川地域支社
AR: MHS Planners, Architects & Engineers　松田平田設計
CD, DD: Yasuhiko Taguchi　田口泰彦
D: Ryo Kusanagi　草梛 亮
DF, SB: Taguchi Design Japan　田口デザインジャパン
P: SS Tokyo　SS東京

JAPAN 2005

Overall signage program for the redevelopment complex (offices, commercial facility, concert hall) and an additional plan for the concert hall. Patterns etc in the signage were developed with a design motif in line with the environmental theme of the whole facility: "feeling the rhythm". Although the form varies from area to area, the facility as a whole has a feeling of cohesiveness by using the same pattern.

再開発複合施設（オフィス棟、商業施設、音楽ホール）における全体サイン計画、および音楽ホールのサイン計画。施設全体の環境演出テーマ「リズムを感じる」に基づくパターンをサインデザインに展開している。それぞれのエリアごとに形態は異なるが、同じパターンを用いることで施設全体の統一感を出した。

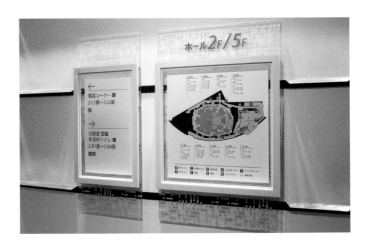

Connect 12 Pedestrian Bridge Network

Commercial Complex　複合商業施設

CL: Hong Kong Land Ltd.
D: David Vanden-Eynden, Principal in Charge, Chris Calori, Advisory Principal, Gina de Benedettis, Designer
AR: Kohn Pedersen Fox Associates, US Architects
AR: LPT Architects, LTD, Hong Kong Architects
SB: Calori & Vanden-Eynden

CHINA 2002

A signage, wayfinding, and branding program for the prestigious 12-building office and retail portfolio covering 20+ blocks of Central, Hong Kong. The goal of the project was to enhance the real estate value by creating an upscale image for the complex network of 10 pedestrian bridges connecting the properties to near by transit nodes and adjoining buildings. Operationally, the project was driven by the bilingual (Chinese and English) signage program, which forms a wayfinding "ribbon" that knits together the complex pathways through the assorted physical characteristics of the various bridges.

香港、セントラル地区のオフィスビル12棟と20以上の商業区域のためのサイン・案内表示・ブランディング・プロジェクト。施設を交通の乗換えの要所や隣接するビル群につなげる10本の歩道橋のイメージを高級化し不動産価値を高めることが目標。中国語・英語表記のサインが複雑な通路と多様な歩道橋を結ぶ「リボン」の役割をはたしている。

Motomachi Cred　基町クレド

Commercial Complex　複合商業施設

CL: NTT Urban Development Co.　NTT都市開発
DD: Shinya Sato　佐藤伸矢
D: Kayo Tamura　田村佳与
DF, SB: Design Soken Hiroshima Inc.　デザイン総研広島
CO: Nomura Co., Ltd.　乃村工藝社
P(ss): Nissho Iwasaki　岩崎日照

JAPAN 2005

Signage upgrade for a ten-year-old commercial complex. The concept of the environmental design was "cool modern". The signage and environmental devices in the lobby are wrapped with "brilliant stripes" (special metallic silkscreen-printed sheets) that emanate a refreshing sparkle. Vivid colors are combined with pictograms that show the facility's functions on a base of monotone stripes.

10周年を迎えた複合商業施設のサインリニューアル。環境デザインのコンセプトは「クールモダン」。爽やかなきらめきを放つブリリアント・ストライプ（メタリックのシルク印刷特注シート）でサインや広場の環境装置を包み込んだ。また、モノトーンのストライプパターンをベースに、施設機能を表すピクトグラムとビビッドなカラーを組み合わせた。

Nihonbashi Mitsui Tower　日本橋三井タワー

Commercial Complex　複合商業施設

CL: Mitsui Fudosan Co., Ltd., Sembikiya　三井不動産　千疋屋総本店
Design Architect: Cesar Pelli & Associates Japan, Inc.　シーザ・ペリ アンドアソシエーツ ジャパン
AR: Nihon Sekkei, Inc.　日本設計
Sign Design: Nihon Sekkei, Inc., Ceser Pelli & Associates Japan, Inc., Rian Ihara Design Office　日本設計
シーザ・ペリ アンドアソシエーツ ジャパン　井原理安デザイン事務所
Sign construction: Kajima Shimizu Mitsuisumitomo Zenitaka Toray Sato JV, Mount Corp., From To Inc, JSP Inc., Tomoe
Inc.　鹿島・清水・三井住友・銭高・東レ・佐藤共同企業体　マウント　フロムトゥ　ジェイエスビー　トモエ
P(ss): Shinichi Tomita　富田眞一　SB: Rian Ihara Design Office　井原理安デザイン事務所

JAPAN 2005

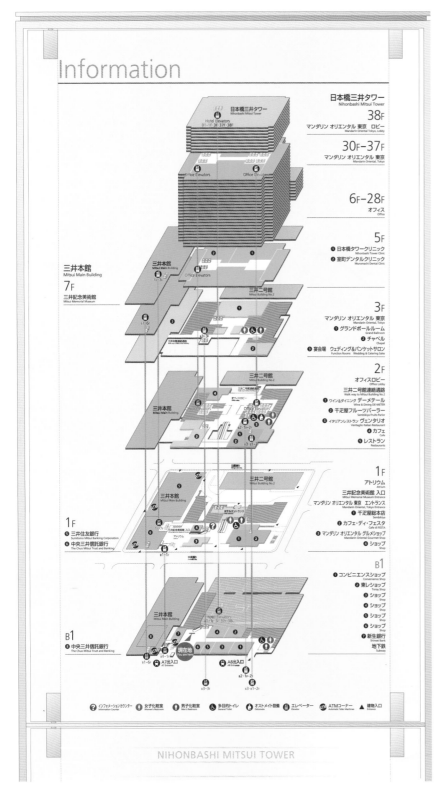

Signage program for Nihonbashi Mitsui Tower, a commercial complex comprising offices, a hotel, and stores. Sign designs were based on six major concepts: 1. Match architectural and spatial scales, 2. Emphasize the vertical linear configuration, 3. Devise effective lighting for both day and night, 4. Make signs functional and user-friendly, 5. Accommodate easy information updates, 6. Utilize glass and metal materials..

オフィス、ホテル、店舗からなる日本橋三井タワーのサイン計画。「1. 建築・空間のスケールにマッチする。2. 縦方向の直線構成を強調する。3. 昼夜における照明効果を図る。4. 利用者にわかりやすく、機能的である。5. 情報の可変性（更新性）が容易である。6. ガラスと金属による構成とする。」という6つの大きなコンセプトのもとにデザインされた。

Nihonbashi 1-Chome Bldg. Coredo Nihonbashi
日本橋一丁目ビルディング　コレド日本橋

Commercial Complex　複合商業施設

CL, S, PR: Mitsui Fudosan Co., Ltd., T-tower　三井不動産　ティタワー
DD: Nihon Sekkei, Inc., Shigeru Sakiyama, Tsugutaka Ikagawa　日本設計　崎山 茂　五十川嗣高
D: Rian Ihara, Toshiaki Yashima　井原理安　八島紀明　DF, SB: Rian Ihara Design Office　井原理安デザイン事務所
CO: Shimizu Sumitomo Mitsui, Tokyu JV, Nomura Coms, Bikohsha Inc.　清水・三井住友・東急建設共同企業体　ノムラコムス
びこう社　AR, Design Architect: Kohn Pederson Fox Associates PC, Nihon Sekkei, Inc., Tokyu Architects & Engineers JV
コーン・ペダーゼン・フォックス・アソシエイツ　日本設計　東急設計コンサルタントJV
P(ss): Shinichi Tomita　富田眞一　　JAPAN　2004

男 性 | 女 性 | オムツ替えシート | どなたでもご利用ください | 授乳室 | サービスセンター
Men | Women | Diaper Changing Table | Free Entry | Nursery | Service Center

定員1名 | エレベーター | エスカレーター | レストラン&カフェ | ショップ | キャッシュサービス
Passing capacity is 1 person | Elevator | Escalator | Restaurants & Café | Shops | ATM Corner

  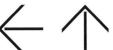 

電話 | 駐車場
Telephone | Parking

複合商業施設

The aim here was to project a clear identity for each facility through office and retail signage in user-friendly designs, based on the building plans. Concepts for the sign design included "materials with an upmarket feel". For office signage, the curvature of the building exterior was incorporated in the shape of the signs, made by bending 40mm-thick sheets of transparent resin, and the arrows placed inside offices designed with the same curve.

設計計画に基づいて、オフィスサイン、商業店舗サインなど各施設のイメージを明確にし、利用者がわかりやすいデザインを目指した。「素材の高級感」などのコンセプトをもとにサインデザインを計画。オフィスサインは建築外観のアールをサイン形態に導入し、厚さ40m/mの透明樹脂板を曲げ、オフィス内に配置する矢印もアールを形どったデザインとした。

Nihonbashi 1-Chome Bldg. Coredo Nihonbashi Parking Lot　日本橋一丁目ビルディング　コレド日本橋駐車場

Commercial Complex　複合商業施設

CL, S, PR: Mitsui Fudosan Co., Ltd., T-tower　三井不動産　ティタワー
DD: Nihon Sekkei, Inc., Shigeru Sakiyama, Tsugutaka Ikagawa　日本設計　崎山 茂　五十川嗣高
D: Rian Ihara, Toshiaki Yashima　井原理安　八島紀明　DF, SB: Rian Ihara Design Office　井原理安デザイン事務所
CO: Shimizu Sumitomo Mitsui, Tokyu JV, Nomura Coms, Bikohsha Inc.　清水・三井住友・東急建設共同企業体　ノムラコムス
びこう社　AR, Design architect: Kohn Pederson Fox Associates PC, Nihon Sekkei, Inc., Tokyu Architects & Engineers JV
コーン・ペダーゼン・フォックス・アソシエイツ　日本設計　東急設計コンサルタントJV　P(ss): Shinichi Tomita　富田眞一
JAPAN 2004

Base color for signage is monotone. Information, wayfinding and graphic signs have a black background with white lettering. Wayfinding instructions are painted directly on the walls in the parking area and car zones A to F are delineated using zone colors. A bright and easy to comprehend parking area for any user.

サインはモノトーンが基調色。案内、誘導、表示系サインは黒ベースに白文字で表現し、駐車場内の壁面ペイントによる誘導表示や車室ゾーン表示は白ベースにA〜Fまでのゾーンカラーを設置。利用者にわかりやすく、明るい駐車場とした。

international finance centre

International Finance Center

Finance Center 金融センター

CL, PC: Central Waterfront Property Project Management (CWPPM)
DD: Ray Parslow
Project Director: Penny Bowring
D: Ray Parslow, Andrea Nixon, Jacqueline Morony, Joanna Mackenzie, Pete Nicholas
DF, SB: Frost Design, Sydney
CO: Photobition Hong Kong, Signhouse Hong Kong
AR: Rocco Design Hong Kong
P(ss): Andrew Loiterton

CHINA 2005

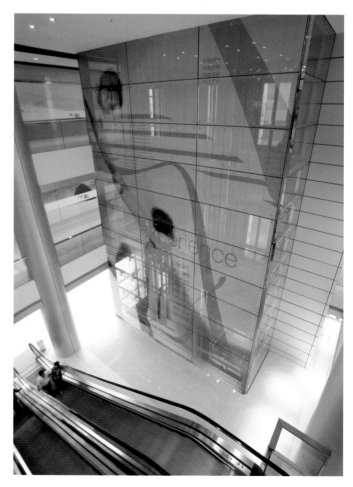

The project involved developing a visual identity for the site and identification and wayfinding graphics and signage for the entire development, as well as large-scale graphic walls. Two forms of identity - corporate and retail - fashioned the wayfinding signage with simple elegant forms that provided clear identification and color palettes that enlivened the signs and coded individual floors. The large-scale graphics make extensive use of color on delicate free-flowing forms reflecting the movement and transparency of the elements, water, earth and sky, adding ambiance to the large voids along circulation routes.

VI、経路案内、施設全体のサイン、大型グラフィック壁等を扱ったプロジェクト。企業用・商用の2種類のVIの必要性から経路案内は簡素で優雅なスタイルとなり、明瞭なVIと色彩が各フロアを演出しつつ区分けしている。水・大地・空の動きと透明感を象徴する繊細で自由な流れの上で効果的な色使いの大きなグラフィックが循環路の周囲を活性化している。

S-ino Omiya　シーノ大宮

Commercial complex　複合ビル

CL: S-ino Omiya　シーノ大宮　鐘塚A地区市街地再開発組合
DF, CO, SB: Kotobuki Corporation　コトブキ
AR: Urban Dynamics Institute Takaha, NTT Facilities Inc.　タカハ都市科学研究所
協力事務所：エヌ・ティ・ティ・ファシリティーズ
P(ss): Shigeru Ohno　大野 繁

JAPAN　2004

A redeveloped complex comprising commercial facilities, business offices and public services. The office sign system utilizes magnetic guide signs, enabling quick and easy changes. Lighting at night for outdoor signs provides helpful wayfinding for visitors.

商業施設、オフィス、公益施設が融合した再開発地区。オフィス棟のガイドサインはマグネットによる着脱式にし、表示内容の変更に素早く対処できるよう留意した。夜にはライトアップされた屋外サインが各施設に誘導してくれる。

Marunouchi OAZO　丸の内オアゾ

Commercial Complex　複合商業施設

CL: Nippon Life Insurance Company, Mitsubishi Estate Co., Ltd., Marunouchi Hotel Co., Ltd.
日本生命保険　三菱地所　丸ノ内ホテル
PC, DD, SB: Mitsubishi Jisho Sekkei　三菱地所設計
D: Rian Ihara Design Office　井原理安デザイン事務所
DF: Mec Design International　メックデザインインターナショナル
CO: Nomura Coms　ノムラコムス

JAPAN 2004

Highly public placement with suitably detailed information was the target of the signage for this city block, which can be accessed from various directions. The aim was a design representing the essence of both the block and Marunouchi. The signs were completed in close liaison with the client.

多方向からのアクセスが可能な当街区のサインは、パブリック性の高い配置と、十分で詳しい情報内容が求められる。クライアントとの綿密な打ち合わせをもとに作りあげたこれらのサインには「街区らしさ」や「丸の内らしさ」を共に演出できるデザインを目指した。

Shiodome City Center　汐留シティセンター

Commercial Complex　複合商業施設

CL: Alderney Investments Pte Ltd., Mitsui Fudosan Co., Ltd.
アルダニー・インベストメンツ・ピーティーイー・リミテッド　三井不動産
S, AR: Nihon Sekkei, Inc.　日本設計
DD: Tetsuichi Tomonaga (T.Glover Co., Ltd.)　朝永徹一（テイ・グラバー）
D: Yuki Ide, Maki Matsuoka (T.Glover Co., Ltd.)　井出由紀　松岡真紀（テイ・グラバー）
DF, CO, SB: T.Glover Co., Ltd.　テイ・グラバー

JAPAN 2003

To make the layout of the complex easier to understand, various colors serve as visual differentiation for the individual zones: common areas, offices, and commercial zones. The commercial zone color contains an element of drama but does not disturb the harmony with the architecture. The information on the signage was arranged considering medium to long-distance legibility. Arrow pictograms made into graphics were widely used to enhance convenience.

複合施設の分類を明確にするため、共用・オフィスゾーンと商業ゾーンに異なるサインカラーを配置し、ゾーンを視覚的に認知させた。商業カラーは演出要素も加味しつつ、建築との調和を乱さないよう選定した。中・遠距離からの可読性を考慮し、表示情報を整理した。また、矢印ピクトをグラフィックとして大きく扱い、利便性の向上を目指した。

Tokyo Twin Parks　東京ツインパークス

Apartment マンション

CL: Mitsubishi Estate Co., Ltd., Mitsui Fudosan Co., Ltd., Sumitomo Reality & Development Co., Ltd. and others
三菱地所　三井不動産　住友不動産　他8社
PC, AR: Mitsubishi Jisho Sekkei Inc. Residential Design & Engineering Department　三菱地所設計 住宅設計部
DD: Isam Sugeno (Mitsubishi Jisho Sekkei Inc. Residential Design & Engineering Department)
菅野 勇(三菱地所設計 住宅設計部)　D: Miyuki Kameya　亀谷美幸　ART, Ceramist: Eisaku Mitsuhashi　三橋英作
CO: Hirose & Co., Ltd.　ヒロセ東京本店　P(ss): Taisuke Ogawa and others　小川泰祐 他
SB: Enviro-System Inc.　エンバイロ・システム

JAPAN　2002

Signage system for a 45-story apartment building in Shiodome. The design of the signage had to be in keeping with the upmarket interiors created by an American designer. Signs were mainly a Japanese ceramic material. Shinshu-ware, with its distinctive glossy red glaze, adds a special accent to the building's spaces, courtesy of ceramic artist Eisaku Mitsuhashi.

汐留に建てられた45階建てマンションのサイン計画。アメリカ人デザイナーの豪華なインテリアにふさわしいサインデザインが求められた。メインは和の素材の陶器で展開。陶芸家三橋英作氏の手による、艶やかな赤が特徴の真朱焼が空間にアクセントを与えている。

Kawaijuku Kojimachi　河合塾　麹町校

College Prep School　予備校

CL: Kawaijuku　河合塾
CD, DD: Yasuhiko Taguchi　田口泰彦
D: Ryo Kusanagi　草柳 亮
DF, SB: Taguchi Design Japan　田口デザインジャパン
P: Miwa Kokyu Photo Laboratory　三輪晃久写真研究所
AR: MHS Planners, Architects & Engineers　松田平田設計

JAPAN 2005

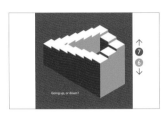

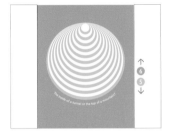

Signage here was mapped out according to the "Life: it gets you thinking" theme for the environment of the facility as a whole. Based on theme colors for each floor, signs employed objects such as clipboards and books, in a design concept befitting a place of learning. The walls of landings on the staircases, which tend usually to be no more than transit points, were designed with graphics using optical illusions, adding color and fun.

施設全体の環境演出テーマ「考えるヒント・いのち」に沿ったサイン計画。各階のテーマカラーをベースに、クリップボードや本を用いたサインを使い、学ぶ場に相応しいデザインとした。また、単なる通行動線になりがちな階段の踊り場の壁面を、錯覚（Optical Illusion）を用いたウォールグラフィックとしてデザインし、空間に彩りと楽しさを作り出した。

Ohnoden Elementary School　武蔵野市立大野田小学校

Elementary School　小学校

CL: Musashino City　武蔵野市
DF, SB, AR: Nihon Sekkei, Inc.　日本設計
AR, CO: Kajima Maruniwatanabe JV　鹿島・丸二渡辺建設共同企業体（建築施工）
CO: Kotobuki Corporation　コトブキ
P(ss): Tokuaki Takimoto　滝本徳明

JAPAN　2005

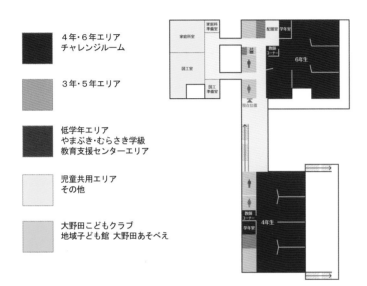

- 4年・6年エリア
  チャレンジルーム

- 3年・5年エリア

- 低学年エリア
  やまぶき・むらさき学級
  教育支援センターエリア

- 児童共用エリア
  その他

- 大野田こどもクラブ
  地域子ども館 大野田あそべえ

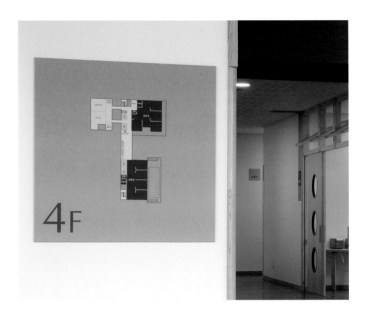

Signage plan for a new school, aiming at creating a special place for the children to call their own while maintaining educational spaces for all areas of learning. Signage was designed in parallel with the new school construction, assigning a theme color to each grade to help students have a feeling of belonging. Signs for special classrooms were adorned with images of the corresponding subject, adding to the affability of the signage.

多様な学習空間に対応できる教育空間であるとともに、子どもたちひとりひとりの居場所を作ることを目指した新校舎のサイン計画。建築と一体化したサインは学年ごとのテーマカラーで統一し、子どもたちが自分たちの居場所として認識する一助となるようデザインされている。特別教室は教科をイメージさせるイラストを用い、親しみの持てるサインとしている。

Schulich School of Business

School of Business　ビジネススクール

CL: Schulich School of Business, York University
S: Dezso Horvath, Dean
PR: Stuart Ash
PC: Justin Young
DD, D: Udo Schliemann
DF, SB: Gottschalk+Ash International
CO: Taylor Manufacturing, King Products, Creative Art Glass
AR: Hariri Pontarini Architects; Robbie / Young+Wright Architects

CANADA 2003

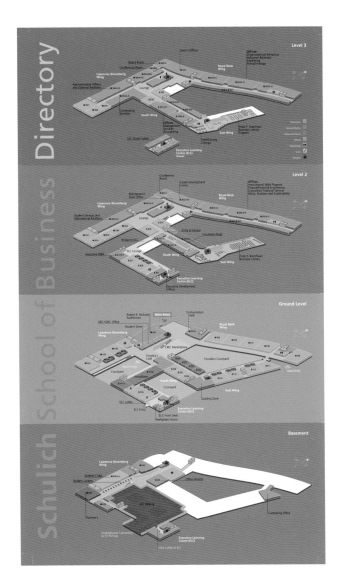

The Schulich School is built around a central "marketplace" with cafe and commons. Hallways lead from the marketplace to quiet research areas and classrooms. The wayfinding program builds on this concept with warm red tones representing the action of the market areas and cool blues for the intimate areas of the school. The signage system uses glass, lighting and color to visually portray this concept throughout the facility, working cohesively with the architect's vision.

シューリック・スクールの建物はカフェ・共有スペース併設の「マーケットプレイス」を中心に研究エリアや教室へと通路がのびる構造。案内表示の基本コンセプトは暖かい赤が市場エリアの躍動感を、涼しげな青がくつろぎの空間を表すというもの。建築家のビジョンにあわせ、サインシステムにはこのコンセプトカラーとガラス、照明が使われた。

Kumamoto Health Science University　熊本保健科学大学

University　大学

CL: Kumamoto Health Science University　熊本保健科学大学
P: Nacása & Partners　ナカサアンドパートナーズ
DF: Koyama　小山
AR, SB: AXS Satow Inc.　佐藤総合計画

JAPAN　2003

The 132m-wide campus is flat, so the emphasis was on configuring the space to make the whole of the building resemble a neighborhood, functioning as a community space. In designing the graphical signs scattered across the white campus, designers were more conscious of how the signs would look to those who see them, than achieving visually attractive proportions. The idea was to make the signage fun for people spending time there, and have it act as a kind of tool for communication.

直径132mのキャンパスはフラットで、建物全体がコミュニティスペースとして機能していく街のような空間構成を重視。白いキャンパスにちりばめたグラフィカルなサインは、見た目のプロポーションの美しさよりも、サインを見た人の目にどう写るかを意識。そこで過ごす人々に楽しさを与え、ひとつのコミュニケーションツールになるよう計画した。

直径132mのキャンパスはフラットで、建物全体がコミュニティスペースとして機能していく街のような空間構成を重視。白いキャンパスにちりばめたグラフィカルなサインは、見た目のプロポーションの美しさよりも、サインを見た人の目にどう写るかを意識。そこで過ごす人々に楽しさを与え、ひとつのコミュニケーションツールになるよう計画した。

Ciclo Básico I-Unicamp

University　大学

CL: Unicamp-University of Campinas
S, DF, SB: t‧h‧e Arquitetura e Design
PC: Paulo de Tarso C. Viana de Souza
DD: Paulo de Tarso C. Viana de Souza e Anelise Ventura
D: Paulo de Tarso C. Viana de Souza, Heloisa Moretzsohn, Anelise Ventura e Fernanda Pedroso

BRAZIL　2003

Located at the Unicamp Campus, one of the most important public universities in Brazil, the Ciclo Basico I complex receives a great many visitors –mainly students, professors and researchers – everyday. The signage plan consists of exterior and interior identification of each building. It also includes some special installations to guide the physically challenged, such as wheelchair signs and Braille messages for children.

ブラジル有数の公立大学UNICAMP（カンピーナス大学）にあるCiclo Basico I は学生、教授、研究者をはじめ非常に多くの人びとが毎日利用する複合施設。そのサインシステムでは、ビルごとの案内が屋内外に設置され、車椅子用の標識や子供向けの点字など身体障害者向けの機能も整えられた。

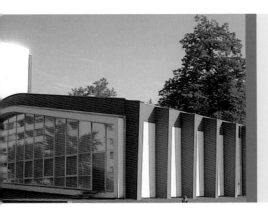

University of Applied Sciences

University 大学

CL: University of Applied Sciences
PC, DD: Sandro Scherling, Reinhard Gassner
D, SB: Sandro Scherling
DF: Saegenvier Designkommunikation+Gassner

AUSTRIA 2002

University of Applied Sciences in Austria. A vast campus found on the outskirts of the city. The signage program provided simple and prominent signs, assigning the facility buildings with letters from A to G.

オーストリアにある応用科学大学内のサイン計画。街の郊外に広大なキャンパスを有している。キャンパス内の各施設をAからGに分けた、わかりやすいサイン。

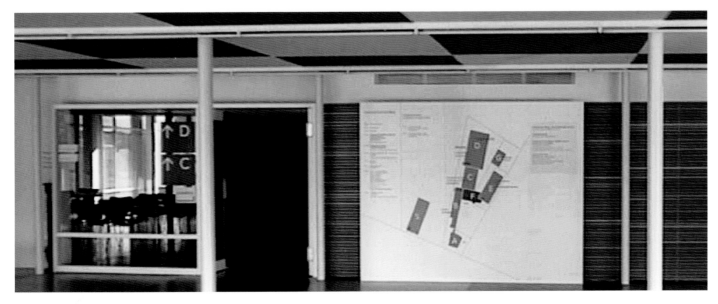

Aichi Shukutoku University Hoshigaoka Campus
愛知淑徳大学　星が丘キャンパス

University　大学

CL: Aichi Shukutoku Gakuen　愛知淑徳学園
S, AR: Nihon Sekkei　日本設計
DD: Kazuo Tomita (Inaryo Technica Co., Ltd.)　冨田一男（稲菱テクニカ）
D: Keiko Shimada (Inaryo Technica Co., Ltd.)　嶋田桂子（稲菱テクニカ）
DF, CO, SB: Inaryo Technica Co., Ltd.　稲菱テクニカ
P(ss): SS Nagoya　SS名古屋

JAPAN　2004

Guide signage installed in the new university buildings of the Aichi Shukutoku Gakuen, which has a proud history of 100 years. The progressive and simple exterior, unified with metal materials such as aluminum, harmonizes with the relaxing atmosphere of the interior space. The aim in the signage program was to create a modern new image, and the design overflows with originality including the notice boards constructed from glass.

創立100年の歴史を誇る愛知淑徳学園の新大学棟に設けられたガイドサイン。アルミ等の金属素材で統一した先進的でシンプルな外観と、落ち着いた空間の内装が調和したデザインとなっている。この計画では現代的な新しいイメージの創出も目指しており、ガラスで構成された掲示板を始め、オリジナリティあふれるピクトグラムもデザインしている。

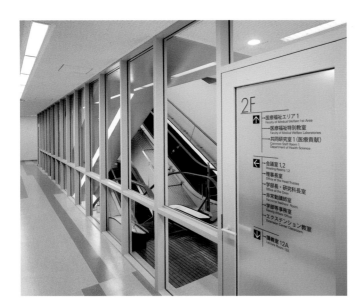

UFRGS

University 大学

CL: UFRGS (Universidade Federal do Rio Grande do Sul)
S: Roberto Bastos
PR: André Renard
PC: Leandra Saldanha
DD: Leonardo Araújo
D: Alessandra Pollo, Karen Berta, Paula Alcaraz Gomes, Roberta Rammé
DF, SB: Gad'design
CO: Soder Engenharia e Construções, Idear System Com Visual

BRAZIL 2004

The challenge of the signage program for the Federal University of Rio Grande do Sul was to create an easily recognizable visual code that valorizes the university's visual identity and at the same time, identifies the accesses and standardizes all visual communication within the parking areas, buildings, rooms, etc, thereby giving uniformity to the different university campuses.

リオ・グランデ・ド・スル連邦大学向けのサインプロジェクト。一目でわかる視覚コードを作成することによって大学のVIを確立すると同時に、構内の移動経路を明確にし、駐車場・建物・教室におけるすべての視覚コミュニケーションを標準化して、複数あるキャンパスに統一感を与えることが目指された。

Meijo University　名城大学

University　大学

CL: Meijo University　学校法人名城大学
P, P(ss): Masaaki Imai　今井正明
DF: Hiromura Design Office, PAS Project Co., Ltd.　廣村デザイン事務所　PAS計画
CO, SB: Kotobuki Corporation　コトブキ
AR: Nikken Sekkei　日建設計

JAPAN　2001

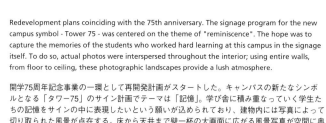

Redevelopment plans coinciding with the 75th anniversary. The signage program for the new campus symbol - Tower 75 - was centered on the theme of "reminiscence". The hope was to capture the memories of the students who worked hard learning at this campus in the signage itself. To do so, actual photos were interspersed throughout the interior; using entire walls, from floor to ceiling, these photographic landscapes provide a lush atmosphere.

開学75周年記念事業の一環として再開発計画がスタートした。キャンパスの新たなシンボルとなる「タワー75」のサイン計画でテーマは「記憶」。学び舎に積み重なっていく学生たちの記憶をサインの中に表現したいという願いが込められており、建物内には写真によって切り取られた風景が点在する。床から天井まで壁一杯の大画面に広がる風景写真が空間に奥行と潤いを与えている。

Aoyama Gakuin University / Sagamihara Campus
青山学院大学　相模原キャンパス

University　大学

CL: Aoyama Gakuin University　青山学院大学
DD, D: Kei Miyazaki (KMD Inc.)　宮崎 桂（ケイエムディー）
CO, SB: Kotobuki Corporation　コトブキ
AR: Nikken Sekkei　日建設計
P(ss): Mikio Kurokawa　黒川未来夫

JAPAN 2003

カラーバーの色相はグループ化され、連続していく。

スポーツ・厚生施設
健康をイメージするグリーン系の色彩

理工学系教室
冷静さをイメージするブルー系の色彩

情報系教室
デジタルをイメージするパープル系の色彩

チャペル
光をイメージするイエローの色彩

文系教室
感情をイメージするオレンジ系の色彩

寮
穏やかさイメージするベージュ系の色彩

New university facilities integrating two separate campuses. Signs were designed for 20 or so buildings using color-coding. The campus sign identity was created using graphical multi-colored bars, unified for both indoor and outdoor signage. The shade of each color varies with each sign, expressing the level of importance within each facility, based on location and contents of the sign.

2つのキャンパスが統合されて新開設された大学。20あまりの施設にはエリアカラーを設定。キャンパスサインのアイデンティティーとして、カラーをグラフィック化した多色カラーバーを屋内や屋外のサインに共通して使用した。各カラーのボリュームはサインごとに変化がつけられ、設置場所と表示内容により異なる各施設の重要度を表現している。

© Mikio Kurokawa

Kanagawa University of Human Services

神奈川県立保健福祉大学

University 大学

CL: Kanagawa Prefecture 神奈川県
DF: PAS Project Co., Ltd. PAS計画
CO, SB: Kotobuki Corporation コトブキ
AR: Tohata Architects & Engineers, Obayashi Corporation 東畑建築事務所 大林組東京本店設計本部
P(ss): Nacása & Partners ナカサアンドパートナーズ

JAPAN 2002

The campus consists of a high-rise block with a long vertical space, and a low-rise block with a separate function, connected by a single large roof. Signage for the campus as a whole has been color-coded to provide clear directions, mindful of where people encounter spaces. The colors of each block, glimpsed from the neutral exterior space, are intended to envelop the buildings.

キャンパスは長い縦空間を持つ高層棟と、独立した機能を持つ低層棟が大屋根で繋がれている。キャンパス全体のサイン計画は、動線を明確にするとともに、空間と人が出会う場面を意識した色彩計画を採用。ニュートラルな外構空間から見え隠れする、各棟の色彩が建物を包み込むことを意図している。

Aichi University Kurumamichi Campus

愛知大学 車道キャンパス

University　大学

CL: Aichi University　愛知大学
DF, CO, SB: Kotobuki Corporation　コトブキ
AR: Nikken Sekkei　日建設計
P(ss): Tokuaki Takimoto　滝本徳明

JAPAN 2004

1F〜4F・13F 一般（パブリック）ゾーン		空 Sky 広い 開けた	
1F〜3F 事務ゾーン		光 Shine 真剣 まなざし	
5F・12F 院生ゾーン		実 Fruitage 実り 成果	
6F 教員（研究）ゾーン		心 Heart 熱心 熱意	
7F〜11F 学生（講義）ゾーン		葉 Green 新鮮 知性	

A newly redeveloped "intelligent city campus" stressing superior law education as well as adult education for residents of the surrounding region. The theme is "Some things change, some things stay the same". As the signs themselves "stay the same," information changeability was integrated into the sign design. The plastic display signs enable quick changes for new information, particularly helping members of the area feel welcome.

高度な法学教育と地域に開かれた社会人教育の拠点として、新しく生まれ変わった都市型インテリジェントキャンパス。テーマは「かわらないもの、かわりゆくもの」。サインは「かわらないもの」として情報を組み合わせたデザインを目指した。また、地域開放に向けて情報の変化に素早く対応するプラズマディスプレイを採用している。

Meiji University Academy Common
明治大学　アカデミーコモン

University　大学

CL: Meiji University Legal Person　明治大学
CO: Kotobuki Corporation　コトブキ
AR, SB: Kume Sekkei Co., Ltd.　久米設計
P(ss): Shigeru Ohno　大野 繁

JAPAN 2004

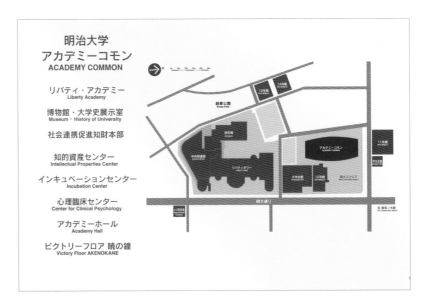

Meiji University Academy Common, with a recently refurbished campus, stresses lifelong learning. Guide signs were created with glass, giving them a transparent feeling to blend in with the architectural design, which aims for both sophistication and openness.

明治大学アカデミーコモンは社会に開かれた生涯学習の拠点として、既存のキャンパスに新築。ガイドサインは品格と開放感の両立を目指した建築デザインと合わせ、透明感のあるガラスを採用した。

The Japanese Red Cross Academy of Narsing

日本赤十字豊田看護大学

University　大学

CL: The Japanese Red Cross Academy of Narsing　日本赤十字学園
PC: Town Art Co., Ltd.　タウンアート
DD: Makoto Takeuchi　竹内 誠
D: Kan Minohara　蓑原 敢
DF, SB: Takeuchidesign Inc.　竹内デザイン
CO: Kotobuki Corporation　コトブキ　AR: Kume Sekkei Co., Ltd.　久米設計

JAPAN 2004

As there was a request from the university for the motif to be a cypress tree, deeply connected to the history of the Red Cross, a logo showing a cypress tree on a hill was proposed and design for the signage that reflected the image of the cypress tree attempted. Color categories were chosen from natural dye colors to clarify facilities in general use such as lecture halls and gymnasiums. This color scheme was also used in a tapestry artwork installed in the university.

クライアントからは、赤十字の歴史に深く関わる「糸杉」をモチーフにしたいとの要望がはじめにあった。そのため、シンボルマークとして丘に立つ糸杉を提案し、サインにも糸杉のイメージを反映するデザインを試みた。一方で、講堂や体育館など一般利用される施設を明快にするため、カラー分類した。配色は自然の染料色から選び、実際に大学に設置されたタペストリー・アートにも使われている。

Hijiyama University Student's Hall　比治山大学学生会館

University　大学

CL: Takenaka, Koujigumi, Nishiki Kensetsu JV　竹中工務店・鴻治組・錦建設共同企業体
PR, DF, CO, SB: Mizma Co., Ltd.　みづま工房
PC: Tsuyoshi Takano　高野 剛
DD, D: Taira Kurisu　栗栖 平
AR: Shirahani Architectural Office　白土建築設計事務所
P(ss): Syuji Satake　佐竹修次

JAPAN　2004

The combination of steel and timber, materials that have a different "feel", expresses "the pleasure of being with friends" and "the tension of learning". Classroom signs that have a tendency to be severe such as on the study rooms were made from wood, which emits a feeling of warmth. Monotone steel was widely used for entrance signage to produce a calmness and functionality.

スチールと木材という素材感が大きく異なる素材の組合せは「仲間と集う楽しみ」と「学ぶ事への緊張感」を表現。また、実習室など硬くなりがちな教室名のサインには、木材を使用することであたたかみを演出。エントランスのサインにはモノトーンのスチールを多く用いることで、落ち着きと機能面を重視したサインとなっている。

Waseda Research Park · Communication Center
早稲田リサーチパーク・コミュニケーションセンター

University　大学

CL: Waseda University　早稲田大学
CO, SB: Kotobuki Corporation　コトブキ
AR: Yamashita Sekkei Inc.　山下設計
P(ss): Katsuhiko Murata (SS Tokyo Co., Ltd.)　村田雄彦（SS東京）

JAPAN 2004

Facility intended as the core of a project to revitalize the surrounding region. The materials and colors used to finish the signage were chosen to match the interior, the idea being to present the signs as part of the building. To convey whether classrooms, use of which is organized according to a flexible system, are occupied, PCs were installed on information signs in a shelving format, allowing viewers to check the signs along with the floor plan on the shelf.

周辺地域の活性化を図る中核拠点として設計された施設。サインを建物の一部として見せることを目指し、サインの仕上げ材・色を内装にあわせた。フレキシブルに変わる教室の使用状況を伝えるため、棚状の総合案内サインにはパソコンが設置され、棚の上面に表示されているフロア案内図とともに確認できるようになっている。

University of Technology, Sydney, Australia

University　大学

CL: University of Technology, Sydney, Australia
PC, CO, P(ss): Signcorp
DD, D: Steven Joseph
DF, SB: Spatchurst

AUSTRALIA 2002

University of Technology Sydney (UTS) is a multi-campus university, with a campus in the inner city and two in Sydney's northern suburbs, and more than 24,000 students enrolled. After reviewing and evaluating existing UTS sign standards, documentation, consultant recommendations and other relevant standards, the new design proposal addressed the issues of corporate image, color, readability, use of maps, reflectivity, typography, structure, location, and the nature of each campus.

シドニー工科大学にはシドニー中心部と郊外に複数のキャンパスがあり、2万4千人以上の学生が在籍。そのサインに関する従来の基準、資料、コンサルタントの提案等を検討、評価した結果、企業イメージ・カラー・可読性・地図の使い方・反射性・タイポグラフィ・建造物・設置位置・各キャンパスの特性等に着目した新デザインが提案された。

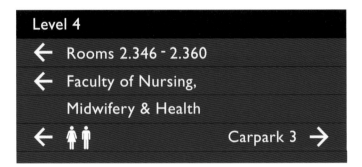

Vale do Rio dos Sinos University

University 大学

CL: Unisinos
S: Valpírio Monteiro
PR: Leandro Giorgetta
PC: Angela Winter, Roberto Bastos
DD: Leonardo Araújo
D: Marcus Padilha, André Lucca, Charles Dröescher, Eduardo Pacheco, André Renard, Gabriel Gallina, Greice Magadan
DF, SB: Gad'design
CO: Huly, Lupa   AR: Márcio Lopes

BRAZIL 2002

The signage program for the Unisinos campus was based on the physical and organizational configuration of the university. The six centers were identified with colors and pictograms creating differentiation as well as a uniform signage system.

バリー・ド・リオ・ドス・シノス大学（UNISINOS）のキャンパス向けサインプロジェクトは、同大学の物理的・組織的構造をベースとしたもの。6つのセンターを色とピクトグラムで識別できると同時に、統一されたサインシステムになっている。

Tokyo University of Agriculture Daiichi High School
東京農業大学第一高等学校

High School 高校

CL: Tokyo University of Agriculture　学校法人東京農業大学
PR: Hiroshi Oyama　大山 博　PC: Akira Fujita　藤田 聡
DD: Yoshiharu Shimura　志村美治　D, P(ss): Eriko Izutsu　井筒英理子
DF, SB: Shimizu Corporation, Field Four Design Office　清水建設　フィールドフォー・デザインオフィス
CO: Shimizu Corporation, To-pro Co., Ltd.　清水建設　東プロ

JAPAN 2003

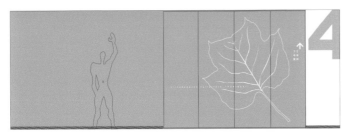

Upgrade program that left most of the existing trees. The signage for the new school buildings used a tree design to give students an opportunity to rethink how wonderful the environment with which they are surrounded is. Room 1F, the teachers' room, was called "Trunk", and Rooms 2, 3 and 4F used by the students were called "Leaves". A signage system where students can use the same classrooms for three years utilizing colors for the building floors was also devised.

多くの既存樹木を残したリニューアル計画。生徒が自分達を取り巻く環境の素晴しさを再確認するきっかけになってほしいと、職員室のある1階を木の「幹」、生徒が使う2、3、4階を木の「葉」と捉え、新校舎のサインに樹木のデザインを採用した。また、階数表示のカラーを生かしつつ、生徒が3年間同じ教室を使うことができるサインシステムを考案した。

Kisarazu National College of Technology

国立木更津工業高等専門学校

College 高等専門学校

CL: Institute of National Colleges of Tecnology, Japan   Kisarazu National College of Technology
独立行政法人 国立高等専門学校機構　木更津工業高等専門学校
CO, SB: Kotobuki Corporation　コトブキ
AR: Nagayama Architechts Co., Ltd.　永山建築設計事務所
P(ss): Tokuaki Takimoto　滝本徳明

JAPAN 2003

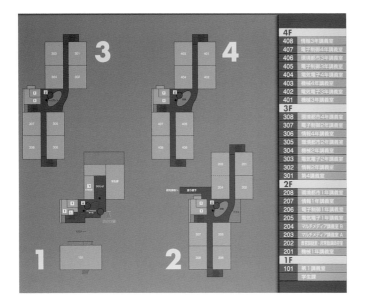

This educational facility turns out highly qualified experts in a wide variety of fields every year. Buildings are basically dark gray, giving a very chic tone. The signage system enables each classroom to exhibit its own changing PR with plastic holders to fit A4-size paper announcements, etc.

数多くの工業分野のエキスパートを排出している教育施設。建物はダークグレーを基調としてシックにまとめた。また、ガイドサインは各教室の特色を自由にPRできるよう、A4サイズの表示内容を簡単に変更できるシステムを採用している。

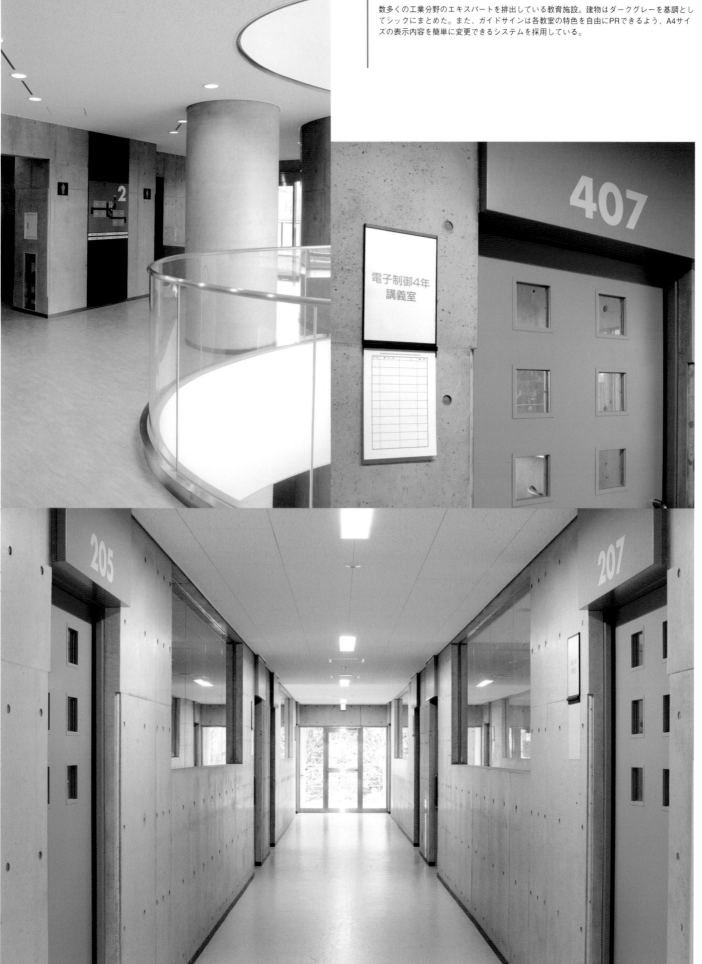

Tokyo Metropolitan Tsubasa Sogo Senior High School
都立つばさ総合高等学校

High School 高等学校

CL: Tokyo Metropolitan Government 東京都
PR: Koichi Ando 安東孝一　DD: Kaoru Kasai 葛西 薫
D: Yasuyuki Ikeda, Yoji Ishii, Mariko Hikichi 池田泰幸　石井洋二　引地摩里子
DF, SB: Sun-Ad Co., Ltd. サン・アド　Text: Toshiyasu Furui 古居利康
AR: Sanichiro Minami 南 三一郎　P(ss): Koichi Aoyama 青山紘一

JAPAN 2002

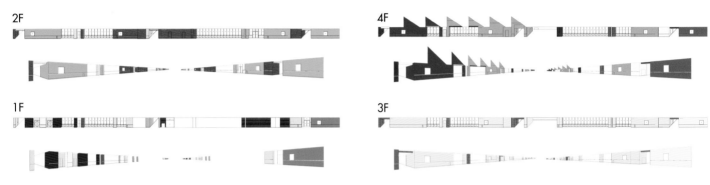

2F

1F

4F

3F

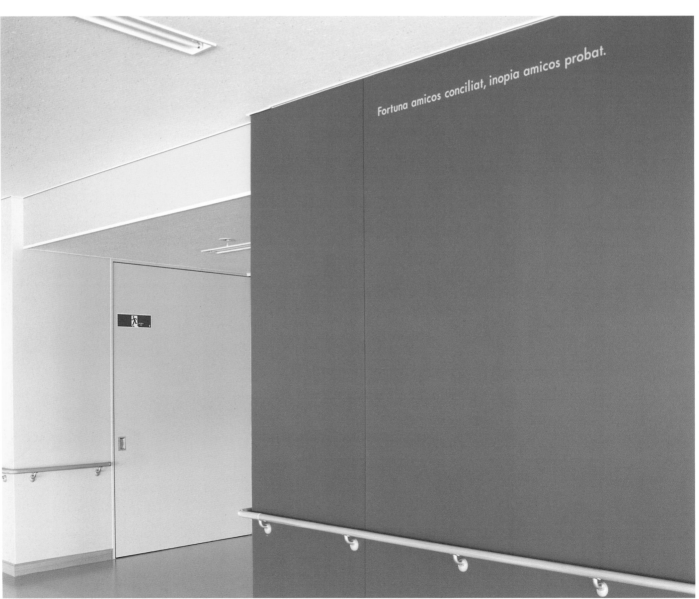

High school with a comprehensive curriculum where subjects with a strong specialist element can be chosen by units. The new school building has an open image not present in traditional schools. Its symbol is "Wisdom on Wall": wall graphics 100 meters in length decorating the walls on each floor. Maxims and wise sayings of the Roman Empire displayed in their original Latin turn the architecture and art of the buildings themselves into teaching materials.

専門色の強い学科を単位で選べる総合学科制の高等学校。新校舎は従来の学校にはない開かれたイメージで設計。そのシンボルになっているのが、全長100mに及ぶ各フロアの壁面に施されたウォールグラフィック「Wisdom On Wall」。古代ローマ文明の箴言、名言を原語のラテン語でレイアウトし、校舎そのものを建築やアートの生きた教材にすることを目指した。

Seiro Middle School　聖籠町立聖籠中学校

Junior High School　中学校

CL: Seiromachi Township　聖籠町
DD: Makoto Takeuchi　竹内 誠
D: Norihiro Matsuo　松尾憲宏
DF, SB: Takeuchidesign Inc.　竹内デザイン
CO: Toda, Shibata, Ishii, Soneken JV　戸田・新発田・石井・曽根建JV
AR: Kohyama Atelier　香山壽夫建築研究所
P(ss): Mitsuru Goto　後藤 充

JAPAN　2001

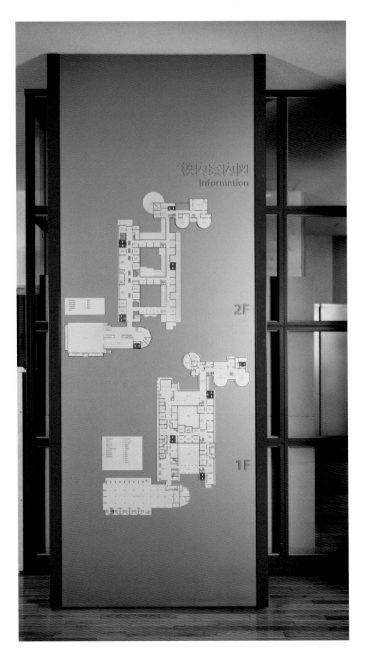

The signage design complements the finish of the building, employing simple shapes and vivid colors. Where signs are placed up high, the display surface is curved and tilted, adding presence and rhythm. It was suggested that symbols thought up by pupils be attached to the names of the main classrooms, so each classroom has a different symbol that is a refined version of ideas that emerged after the children had been to a graphic design lesson.

サインデザインは、建築の仕上げと呼応してシンプルな形状とビビッドな色彩を採用。取り付け位置が高い場所には表示面をアールにして傾斜させ、存在感とリズムを与えた。主な教室名には「生徒達で考えたマークを付けてはどうか？」という提案により、グラフィックデザインの授業を行って出てきたアイデアをリファインした、教室のマークが設定されている。

Nakagawamachi-kita Junior High School
那珂川北中学校

Junior High School　中学校

CL: Nakagawamachi　那珂川町
S, PR, AR: Teruaki Tomisawa (Kumesekkei)　富沢照秋（久米設計）
PC, DD: Toshihiro Yamamoto (Hadakogeisha)　山本俊祐（ハダ工芸社）
D, P, P(ss): Hitomi Ishikawa (Hadakogeisha)　石川ひとみ（ハダ工芸社）
DF, CO, SB: Hadakogeisha　ハダ工芸社　CO: Chikara Sawazaki (Hadakogeisha)　澤崎 力（ハダ工芸社）

JAPAN 2004

Junior high school built in response to the population increase in a new residential development. The signage program makes strong use of "color", mainly primary, to accent the facility interior. Different colors were selected for each floor and applied to all items to give each floor a distinct identity. Signage creating a fun atmosphere using pictograms and typefaces and conscious of the age group of users was achieved.

新興住宅地の人口増加に伴い新設された中学校。サイン計画は内装でのアクセントをテーマに、主に原色を用いた「色」を全面に展開。それぞれフロアカラーを選定し、色彩による階層の認識ができるよう、すべてのアイテムにフロアカラーの色彩展開を行った。さらにピクトデザインや書体など、施設主利用者の年齢層を意識した楽しい雰囲気のサインを実現した。

Numazu Ichiritsu Numazu High School / Junior High School
沼津市立沼津高等学校・中等部

High School, Junior High School 高校・中学校

CL: Numazu City 沼津市
S, AR: Rui Sekkeishitsu 類設計室
DD: Susumu Sugitani 杉谷 進
D: Susumu Sugitani, Miho Saito 杉谷 進 齋藤美帆
DF: Zuco-can 図考館 CO, SB: Kotobuki Corporation コトブキ
P(ss): Tokuaki Takimoto 滝本徳明

JAPAN 2002

Designed in anticipation that opening the school up to the community would result in community and school activities capitalizing on each other, inspiring and stimulating the children. This concept was extended to the signs, which not only show the names of different spaces, but feature stylized characters that conjure up images of the activities taking place there.

地域に開放することで地域と学校の活動が互いに生かされ、生徒達の活力につながることを期待して設計されている。サインも単に空間の名称を表示するだけでなく、「福祉」の文字には部首に駆け足する人の躍動感、ハートとケアに携わる家を組み入れるなど、文字をデフォルメしたデザインを施し、そこでの活動がイメージできる形を作りあげた。

Hospital Moinhos de Ventos (Sinalizacao Park)

Rehabilitation Park　リハビリパーク

CL: Hospital Moinhos de Ventos
S: Janaína Duarte
PR: André Renard
PC: Leandra Saldanha
DD: Leonardo Araújo
D: Alessnadra Pollo
DF, SB: Gad'design
CO: Lupa, Durapine

BRAZIL 2004

The signage program promoting Moinhos de Ventos Hospital's disease prevention program and encouraging physical exercise was designed to identify walking paths and provide information on exercising and health habits. Wood was used as a primary element to integrate the signage into the natural environment of the park.

モインホス・デ・ベントス病院 の疾病予防プロジェクトの推進と、運動奨励のためのサイン。歩行用通路の案内や運動・健康習慣に関する情報提供を目指してデザインされている。サインが公園の自然環境に溶け込むよう、主に木材を使用。

Children's Hospital Boston

Hospital 病院

PC: David Gibson
DD: Anthony Ferrara
D: Alexandra Lee, Dominic Borgia
SB: Two Twelve Associates

USA 2004

Of special concern in the analysis of the hospital's signage needs and the design of appropriate solutions was that the signage be clear, attractive and communicate to the multicultural users of this major healthcare facility. To appeal to the children's sense of wonder, as well as serve as a wayfinding tool, a series of color-coded, alliterative icons were developed, one for each building, which were then applied throughout the wayfinding program, on directories and directional and identification signs.

この病院に必要かつ適切なデザインを分析したところ、わかりやすく、楽しく、大病院ならではの患者の多民族性に対応したものにすることに焦点があたった。子ども達の興味をひきつつ、案内ツールとしても機能するよう、ビルごとに色分けされた象徴的なアイコンが、標識・方向指示・各施設や設備の表示など、館内全体に使用された。

Pediatrico Center of the Lagoon

Clinic 診療所

CL, PR: Centro Pediátrico da Lagoa
PC: Valéria London
DD: Valéria London, Ana Lúcia Velho
D: Atsuhiko Hiratsuka, Luciana Gutiérrez, Claudia Gutwilen
P: Marcos Morteira
DF, SB: Valéria London Design

BRAZIL 1999

Less pain, less suffering. The design project for this children's hospital aimed to provide an element of comfort and relief and the environmental graphics are integrally related to this central concept. Nature was the adopted theme, with each ground treated as part of the natural environment: sea, earth, sky and space. Family and tenderness represented in the brand, while the little birds (boy and girl) were conceived to be used as three-dimensional pets to help children to face illness more easily.

痛みや苦しみを少なく。小児科病院のサインプロジェクトでは快適さと安らぎを表現することが目指された。自然をテーマに、各エリアを 海、地球、空、宇宙などの自然環境の一部として扱っている。デザインでは家族と優しさが描かれると同時に子どもが病気に立ち向かいやすくなるよう、小鳥（オスとメス）を立体感のあるサインとして使用。

Narita Cityu Health & Welfare Center　成田市保健福祉館

Hospital　病院

CL: Narita City　成田市
PR, AR: Tohata Architects & Engineers　東畑建築事務所
PR: Yutaka Kawahara　河原 泰
DF, CO, SB: Kotobuki Corporation　コトブキ
P(ss): Tokuaki Takimoto　滝本徳明

JAPAN 2002

A traditional Japanese-style architecture: wooden terraced construction and tiled roofing, allowing the building to exude the warmth of the wood. The key point in the architecture was a universal design making the facility a comfortable and welcome place for everyone, especially the elderly and disabled. Signage was created to match the architecture, using traditional Japanese paper to give off a gentle impression. Animal characters adorn room signs and the general information sign at the entrance was designed to be user-friendly and easy to understand.

木の温もりを生かした木造平屋建て、瓦葺きの日本建築。子ども、高齢者、障害者など誰もが安心して利用できるユニバーサルデザインに重点を置いた。サインも建築のデザインに合わせ、優しい印象の和紙を使用。室名サインには動物のキャラクターを採用し、入口の総合案内サインもわかりやすくするなど、誰にでも利用しやすいように配慮した。

The Scarborough Hospital

Hospital　病院

CL: The Scarborough Hospital
S: Wayne McCutcheon
Producer of Signage: WSI Signs
PC: Bryan Wallis
DD: Veronica Chan
D: Veronica Chan, John Pereira
P, P(ss): Kerun IP
DF, SB: Entro Communications

CANADA　2005

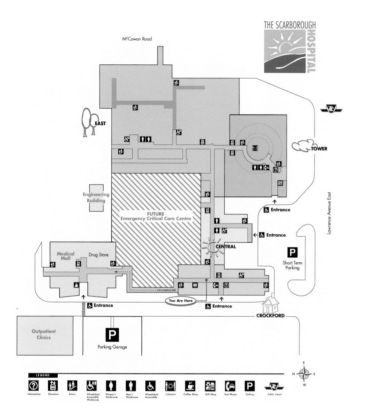

Ongoing changes to The Scarborough Hospital's plan created a need for a comprehensive wayfinding program for the 470,000 sq.ft. healthcare facility. In consideration of the hospital's location within a multicultural community, design of the wayfinding system incorporated three basic elements: names, colors and icons. Elements of the system included a bright color palette, and separate identities for each wing. Simple and generic graphic icons – cloud, tree, sun and house – formed easily recognizable signatures and created a visual liveliness for each wing.

スカーバラ病院の改修で約4万3千660平方メートルの施設の総合案内システムの構築が求められた。病院が多民族地域にあることから、名前・色・アイコンという基本3要素に加え、明るい配色と各棟の区別がデザインの要件となった。雲、木、太陽、家というシンプルで一般的なアイコンにより、わかりやすく、いきいきとしたサインが棟ごとに設置された。

National Center for Child Health and Development
国立成育医療センター

Hospital　病院

CL: National Center for Child Health and Development　国立成育医療センター
S, AR: Dept. of National Hospital, Ministry of Health, Labor & Welfare, Nikken Sekkei, NIKKEN SPACE DESIGN Ltd.,
Mitsuru Senda+Enviroment Design Institute　厚生労働省健康局国立病院部経営指導課　日建設計　日建スペースデザイン
仙田満+環境デザイン研究所　CO: Kotobuki Corporation, Central Uni Co., Ltd., NOMURA Co., Ltd. (Japanese Lexial
Order)　コトブキ　セントラルユニ　乃村工藝社（アイウエオ順）
P(ss): Mikio Kurokawa　黒川未来夫

JAPAN 2004

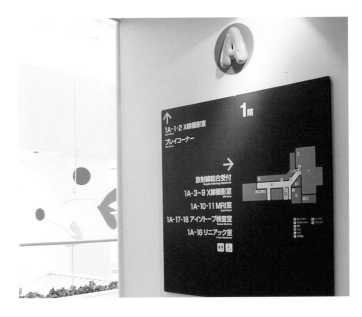

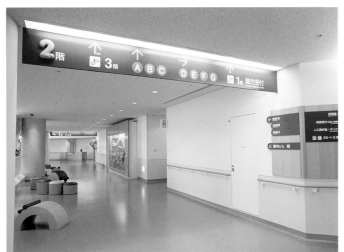

New facility established to take on pediatric, maternal and paternal medicine and continuous medical treatment in related areas. The signage and artwork respectively have been designed to create an intelligible and fun environment for kids while fulfilling their role.

小児医療から母性・父性医療、および関連領域を包括する継続的医療を担う施設として新設。サイン計画は、子どもにもわかりやすく楽しい環境を作り出すよう、サインとアートそれぞれの役割を生かしながらトータルにデザインされている。

©Mikio Kurokawa

Satoh Hospital　佐藤病院

Hospital　病院

CL: Misugikai　医療法人 美杉会
PR, SB: Kajima Design Kansai　鹿島建設 関西支店 建築設計部
PC: Toru Hamada　浜田 徹
DD: Naotaka Obayashi　大林直高
D: Michiya Ono　小野道也
P: Akiyoshi Fukuzawa　福澤昭嘉

JAPAN　2002

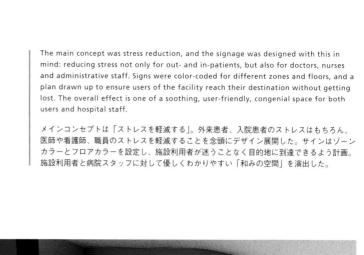

The main concept was stress reduction, and the signage was designed with this in mind: reducing stress not only for out- and in-patients, but also for doctors, nurses and administrative staff. Signs were color-coded for different zones and floors, and a plan drawn up to ensure users of the facility reach their destination without getting lost. The overall effect is one of a soothing, user-friendly, congenial space for both users and hospital staff.

メインコンセプトは「ストレスを軽減する」。外来患者、入院患者のストレスはもちろん、医師や看護師、職員のストレスを軽減することを念頭にデザイン展開した。サインはゾーンカラーとフロアカラーを設定し、施設利用者が迷うことなく目的地に到達できるよう計画。施設利用者と病院スタッフに対して優しくわかりやすい「和みの空間」を演出した。

KKR Keihanna Hospital
国家公務員共済組合連合会　KKR京阪奈病院

Hospital　病院

CL: KKR Keihanna Hospital　国家公務員共済組合連合会　KKR京阪奈病院
DF: Emotional Space Design　エモーショナル・スペース・デザイン
CO, SB: Kotobuki Corporation　コトブキ
P(ss): Tokuaki Takimoto　滝本徳明

JAPAN 2004

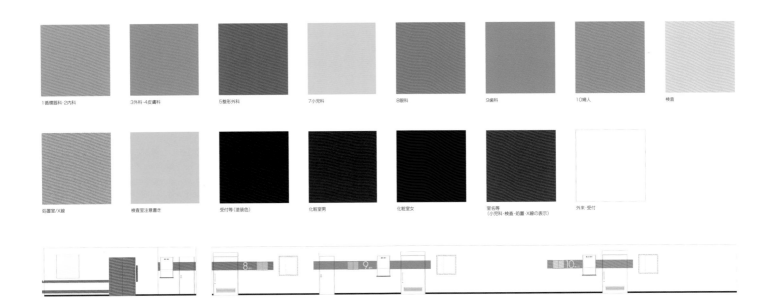

1循環器科・2内科　　3外科・4皮膚科　　5整形外科　　7小児科　　8眼科　　9歯科　　10婦人　　検査

処置室/X線　　検査室注意書き　　受付等（塗装色）　　化粧室男　　化粧室女　　室名等（小児科・検査・処置・X線の表示）　　外来・受付

Project to update guide signs. Distinctive banded signs were introduced to make signs easier to understand, and impart a fresh, up-to-date look. The ability to read information on the different departments without raising or lowering one's line of sight greatly improved the legibility of the signs. Colors are bright and easy on the eye.

ガイドサインのリニューアル。帯状の特徴的なサインを導入することで、よりわかりやすく、新しい印象を与えた。目線の高さを変えることなく各診療科の情報が理解できるため、ガイドサインの見やすさは飛躍的に向上した。カラー計画は明るく、しかも目に優しい風合いの色を採用した。

Yuzawa Community Medical Center
湯沢町保健医療センター

Hospital　病院

CL: Yuzawa Town　湯沢町
CO, SB: Kotobuki Corporation　コトブキ
AR: NTT Facilities Inc.　エヌ・ティ・ティ・ファシリティーズ
P(ss): Tokuaki Takimoto　滝本徳明

JAPAN 2002

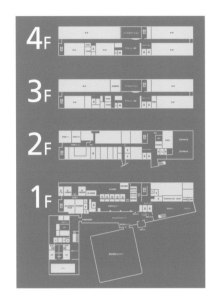

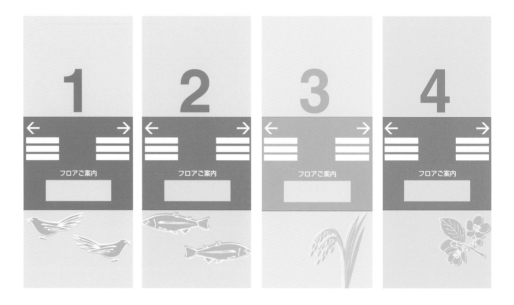

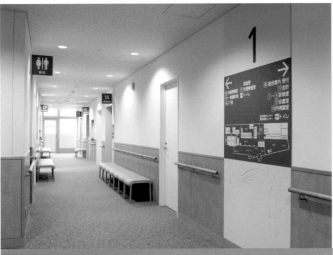

In the signage system, theme colors and character symbols were set for each floor, based on aspects of the natural environment familiar to local residents. The color plan for the first and second floor outpatient areas was designed to give the facilities a bright, upbeat look with minimal clutter by, for example, adding white lighting; in contrast, color and lighting combinations for the wards, on the third and fourth floors, were chosen for their warmth.

サイン計画では街になじみのある《自然》をテーマに、各階にテーマカラーとシンボルキャラクターを設定。1、2階の外来エリアは照明も白色系を合わせるなど、すっきりとした明るい印象の色彩計画を採用。それに対し、3、4階の病棟フロアは色彩・照明ともにあたたかな印象の組み合わせが選ばれた。

Aso Iizuka Hospital　麻生飯塚病院

Hospital　病院

CL: Aso Iizuka Hospital　麻生飯塚病院
S, PR: Akimi Furuhata (Ishimoto)　古畠安紀美 (石本建設事務所)
PC, AR: Naoya Okuda (Kajima Design Kyushu)　屋田直哉 (KAJIMA DESIGN Kyushu)
DD: Toshihiro Yamamoto (Hadakogeisha)　山本俊祐 (ハダ工芸社)
D, P, P(ss): Hitomi Ishikawa (Hadakogeisha)　石川ひとみ (ハダ工芸社)
CO: Sanshiro Yao (Hadakogeisha)　八尾三四郎 (ハダ工芸社)
SB: Hadakogeisha　ハダ工芸社

JAPAN　2004

General hospital that serves both as an emergency and an oncology ward on a vast site in Iizuka, a former coal-producing region. The basic color palette was selected for its qualities of "healing" and "tranquility" and to contrast the background color covering the surface of the signage. As well, sprinkling artwork around the circumference added to the therapeutic and peaceful atmosphere.

旧産炭地・飯塚にある広大な敷地の総合病院内の救急と癌治療を兼ねた病棟。基本色は「癒し」や「安らぎ」を感じさせる色の選定にこだわり、サイン全面に基本色のコントラストを展開した。また周囲にアートワークを点在させることで、癒しと安らぎの空間を演出している。

Tama Neurosurgery Clinic　多摩脳神経外科

Clinic　診療所

CL: Kazuo Isayama (Tama Neurosurgery Clinic)　諫山和男（多摩脳神経外科）
S, DD: Takeyuki Uchida (Exas Inc.)　内田武之（エクサス）
DF: Exas Institute Inc.　エクサス研究所
CO: Kobayashi Kogei-Sha Co., Ltd.　小林工芸社
AR, SB: Exas Inc.　エクサス

JAPAN 2001

The Tama Neurosurgery Clinic opened as a first stop for chronic problems arising from the stresses of modern living, such as headaches and aching back and neck muscles. The brain design of the clinic's logo is a stylized version of the signature letter "I" used by the clinic's director Dr. Isayama, a clear statement of his status as a specialist of 20 years standing in the treatment of stroke patients.

多摩脳神経外科は、ストレスの多い現代人の頭痛や肩こりなどの慢性的な悩みに対応するかかりつけの医院として誕生。シンボルマークになっている脳の図案は、院長諫山氏のイニシャル「I」が図案化されており、20年にわたる脳卒中治療の専門医としてのアイデンティティを明確に表現している。

Takeda General Hospital / Yamaga Clinic
財団法人竹田綜合病院 山鹿クリニック

Hospital　病院

CL: Takeda General Hospital　財団法人竹田綜合病院
S: Nihon Healthcare Techno Inc.　日本ヘルスケアテクノ
DF: Archidesign & Partners Co., Kotobuki Corporation　アーキデザイン研究所　コトブキ
CO, SB: Kotobuki Corporation　コトブキ
AR: Nihon Healthcare Techno Inc. Archidesign & Partners Co.　日本ヘルスケアテクノ（総合企画）アーキデザイン研究所
P(ss): Nacása & Partners　ナカサアンドパートナーズ

JAPAN 2002

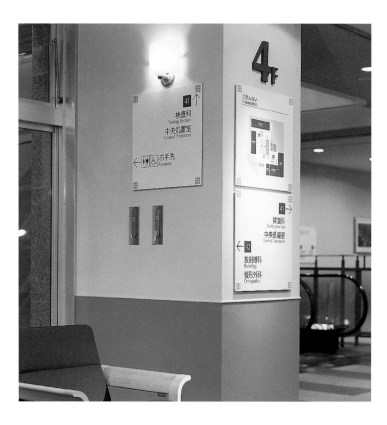

インテリア		
7F	リラクゼーション	
6F	診療・検査 （産科・婦人科）	**Wellness** エレガントカラー
5F		
4F	診療・検査（その他）	**Clinic** ナチュラルカラー
3F		
2F	スタッフフロア	
1F	パブリックフロア （受付・店舗）	**Urban** ニュートラルカラー

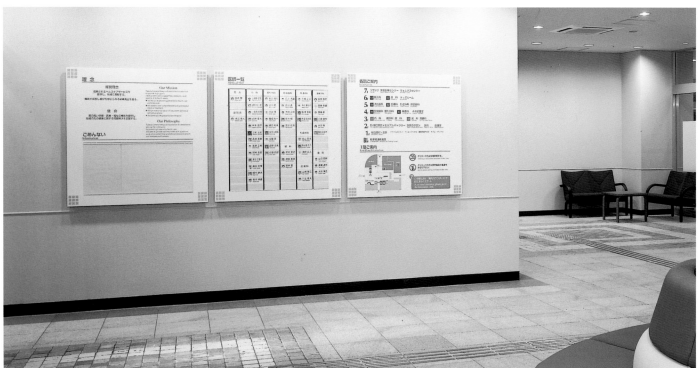

A guide sign program created to match the colors of the interior, yet designed with varying subtle shades so as not to become too monotone and stale. The signs were kept simple, maintaining an unobtrusive presence while entwining with the lighting to improve visibility and create a comfortable atmosphere.

ガイドサインはインテリアカラーに合わせて計画。単調になりすぎないよう、微妙な色調とボリュームでデザインした。また、サインの存在をできるだけ抑えシンプルに、さらに照明と絡ませながら誘目性を高めることで、空間と調和させることを目指した。

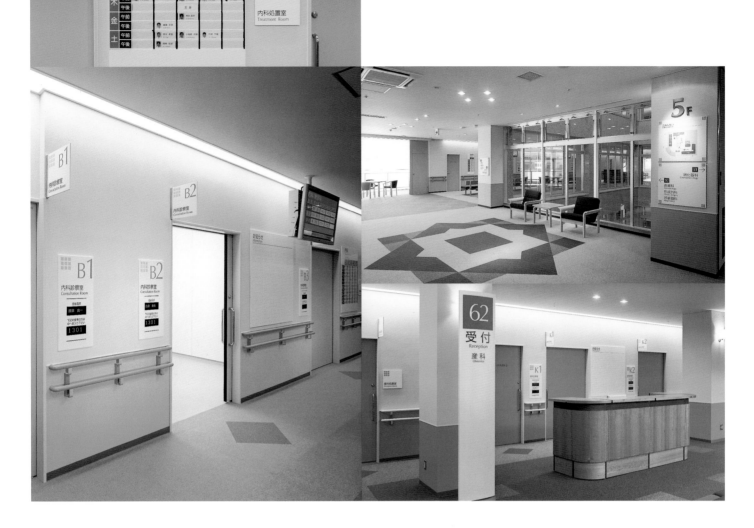

Tazawako Hospital　仙北市立田沢湖病院

Hospital　病院

CL: Semboku City　仙北市
DF, AR: Nikken Sekkei　日建設計
CO, SB: Kotobuki Corporation　コトブキ
P(ss): Shigeru Ohno　大野 繁

JAPAN 2003

2F

誘導			管理部門
ガーデンホール			病室

1F

誘導			管理部門
外来部門			健康増進センター

りんどう

しゃくなげ

うめ

ふじ

すずらん

みずばしょう

In keeping with the shades of the wooden building materials used in the interior, the signage program was devised with a low color-saturation level involving only four colors. Each color was categorized per function and graphic designs were aimed at keeping a fresh look using the four colors accordingly. The architectural module signs were matched with the modules to create a formation that puts both visitors and users at ease.

サイン計画はインテリアの木材の色調に合わせ、彩度の低い4色のカラーを設定。それぞれの機能に合わせて使い分け、色を組み合わせることで単調にならないようなグラフィックデザインを目指した。また、建築のモジュールサインと、モジュールを合わせることで、空間になじみやすいように構成している。

Kyushu Kousei Nenkin Hospital

財団法人厚生年金事業振興団　九州厚生年金病院

Hospital　病院

CL: Fukuoka Social Insurance Bureau　福岡社会保険事業局
D, AR: Hiroshi Mizuguchi　水口弘志
DF: Envics.　エンビックス
CO, SB: Kotobuki Corporation　コトブキ
AR: Nikken Sekkei　日建設計
P(ss): Shigeru Ohno　大野 繁

JAPAN 2004

Signage largely using artistic graphics, called marker signs, is incorporated ubiquitously throughout the underlying architectural atmosphere of brick, tile and wood materials, bringing change to the entire space. The graphics differ with each floor. Marker signs indicating specific floors are placed in front of elevators. Guidance signs and patient room signs have a common graphic thread, bringing a sense of unity within in each hospital wing.

れんがやタイルや木を基調とした建築空間の中で随所に「目印サイン」と称しているアート的なグラフィックを大きく扱ったサインが盛り込まれ、空間に変化を与えています。グラフィックはフロアによって異なっています。エレベーターは正面にはフロアを印象付ける目印サインを設置。誘導サインと病室サインにもグラフィックに共通性を持たせ、病棟内の統一感を出しています。

Tohno Kosei Hospital　JA岐阜厚生連　東濃厚生病院

Hospital　病院

CL: JA Gifu Kouseiren　JA岐阜厚生連
DF: PAS Project Co., Ltd.　PAS計画
CO, SB: Kotobuki Corporation　コトブキ
AR: Zen-Noh Architects & Engineers Inc.　全国農協設計
P(ss): Shigeru Ohno　大野 繁

JAPAN　2004

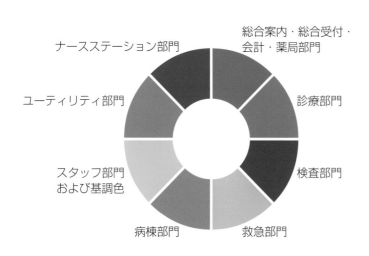

ナースステーション部門
総合案内・総合受付・
会計・薬局部門
ユーティリティ部門
診療部門
スタッフ部門
および基調色
検査部門
病棟部門
救急部門

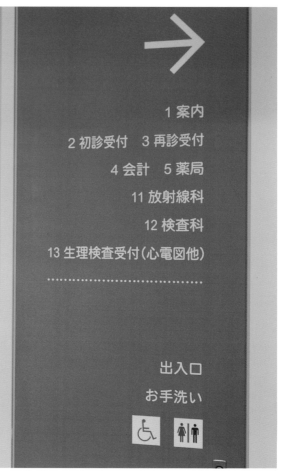

The hospital was divided into eight blocks, such as the information desk, accounts department, consultation and treatment section, and laboratories, and a different color used for each to facilitate the smooth movement of patients around the hospital. For the blocks with the highest volume of traffic, Gifu prefectural flowers, the bellflower and star magnolia, were selected as eye-catching motifs to provide even clearer wayfinding.

総合案内・会計部門、診療部門、検査部門ほか8つのブロックに病院を分け、それぞれの色（ブロックカラー）を採用。これにより、院内での患者の移動をスムーズに誘導できるようになった。また、特に利用頻度の高いブロックには、岐阜県の花であるキキョウとシデコブシをアイキャッチとして選定。さらに明確な誘導のサポートとなった。　医療施設

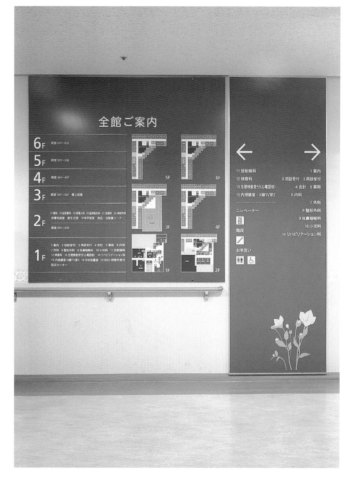

Tohya Hospital　社会福祉法人 北海道社会事業協会 洞爺病院

Hospital　病院

CL: Tohya Hospital　社会福祉法人 北海道社会事業協会 洞爺病院
CO, SB: Kotobuki Corporation　コトブキ
AR: Yamashita Sekkei Inc.　山下設計
P(ss): Tokuaki Takimoto　滝本徳明

JAPAN 2003

A hospital that treats both acute diseases and chronic illnesses, focusing mainly on rehabilitation treatment, offering a nexus of reassurance for local residents. Each ward is named after a regional flower and a point illustration has been incorporated into the signage producing a soft and gentle effect.

リハビリテーション医療を中心に、急性疾患、慢性疾患の両方に対応した地域住民の安心の要となっている病院。院内の誘導サインには各病棟の名前ともなっている、地元の花をモチーフにしたポイントイラストが入り、やわらかく優しい雰囲気を演出している。

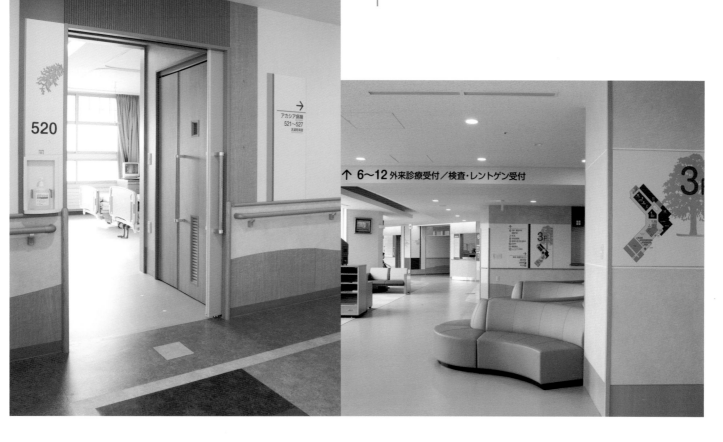

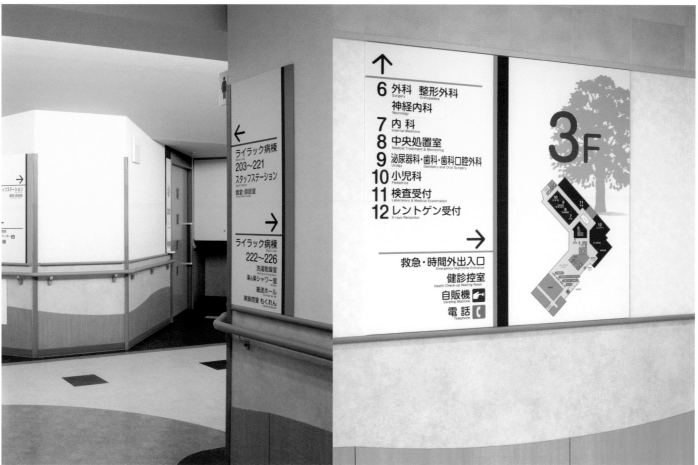

Sayama General Hospital
医療法人財団石心会　さやま総合クリニック

Hospital　病院

CL: Sayama General Hospital　医療法人財団石心会 さやま総合クリニック
DF, CO, SB: Kotobuki Corporation　コトブキ
AR: Ray Architects　玲設計
P(ss): Shigeru Ohno　大野 繁

JAPAN 2003

各フロアの イメージ

 5F こころ 心　管理部門

 4F ひかり 光　透析室

 3F とり 鳥　外来診療

 2F はな 花　外来診療

 1F みどり 緑　総合受付・会計 検査部門

The slogan here was "creating a warm and welcoming environment". On the third floor a grand piano has been installed for a program of "healthy concerts" open to local people free of charge. The base color for the signage is green, inspired by the tea that is a Sayama specialty. The exits on each floor feature motifs from nature such as sky or land, while the shin (heart) of Sekishinkai has been employed for the administrative section on the top floor.

スローガンは「あったか環境づくり」。3階にはグランドピアノを置き、地域の方々が無料でコンサートを楽しめる「ヘルシーコンサート」を企画。サイン計画は狭山特産のお茶をイメージしたグリーンがベースカラー。各フロアの降り口に、大地や空などの自然をモチーフとしたイラストを設置。また、最上階の管理部門は石心会の「心」をモチーフとした。

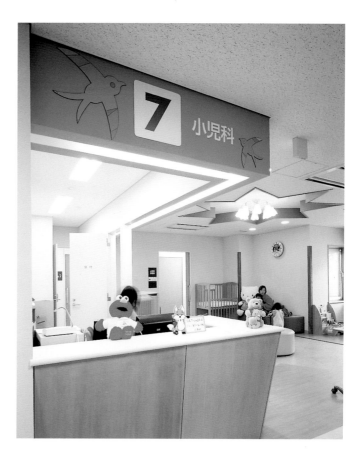

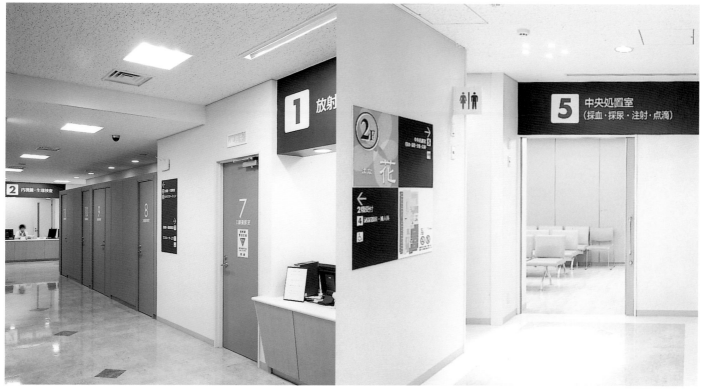

Kurashiki Central Hospital　倉敷中央病院

Hospital　病院

CL: Kurashiki Central Hospital　財団法人倉敷中央病院
DF, CO, SB: Kotobuki Corporation　コトブキ
AR: UR Sekkei　UR設計医療福祉施設研究室
P(ss): Tokuaki Takimoto　滝本徳明

JAPAN 2002

A hospital with approximately 80 years of rich history. Landmark signs include old-fashioned postboxes and birdcages. With aims to create a smooth wayfinding system for outpatients, floor numbers and room numbers are displayed in blocks clearly indicating purposes, such as "Medical Department" and "Medical Exams". Sign plates are decorated with graphics of ornamental plants and ivy, echoing the floral arrangements found adorning the hospital at every corner.

約80年の歴史を持つ病院。ランドマークサインとして旧型のポストや鳥かごを設置。また、外来ではスムーズな誘導を目指し、「診療科目」「検査」などブロック単位で階数表示と通し番号で表記した。サインの基板には、院内のレリーフなどでも随所に盛り込まれている観葉植物・アイビーをモチーフとして使用した。

アイビーの
モチーフ

通し番号
ブロック表示
階数表示

Massachusetts General Hospital

Hospital 病院

CL: Massachusetts General Hospital
S: Barbara Welanets Planning and Construction Office
PC: David Gibson
DD: Anthony Ferrara
D: Yanira Hernandez, Pamela Paul, Dominic Borgia
DF, SB: Two Twelve Assocaites, Inc.

USA 2004

A wayfinding system that builds upon the unified network of corridors and lobbies that wind throughout this large campus of eighteen buildings. The new program provides a series of routes and stops that work like a mass transit system, helping people locate their destinations while they are still on the ground floor. The color-coded signage system relates to the hospital's existing building address system: each building name corresponding to a specific color. A series of banners represent the diverse, welcoming nature of the hospital community.

18棟からなる巨大な施設内の廊下とロビーの迷路に設置された案内システム。新プロジェクトでは公共の交通サインと同様のシステムを廊下と広場の道案内に採用。1階にいても目的の場所を突き止めることが可能になった。サインは既存の病棟内放送システムにそって病棟ごとに色分けされている。各標識がこの病院の多様性と友好的ムードを表現。

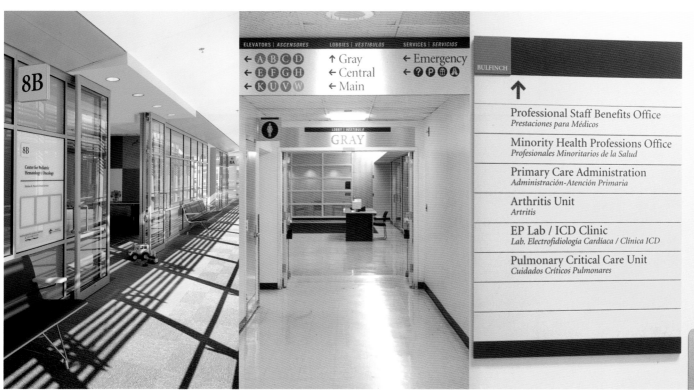

Ebina Medical Plaza
特定医療法人ジャパンメディカルアライアンス　海老名メディカルプラザ

Hospital　病院

CL: Japan Medical Alliance　特定医療法人ジャパンメディカルアライアンス
DF: Irie Miyake Architects & Engineers, Kotobuki Corporation　入江三宅設計事務所　コトブキ
CO, SB: Kotobuki Corporation　コトブキ
AR: Irie Miyake Architects & Engineers　入江三宅設計事務所
P(ss): Shigeru Ohno　大野 繁

JAPAN 2005

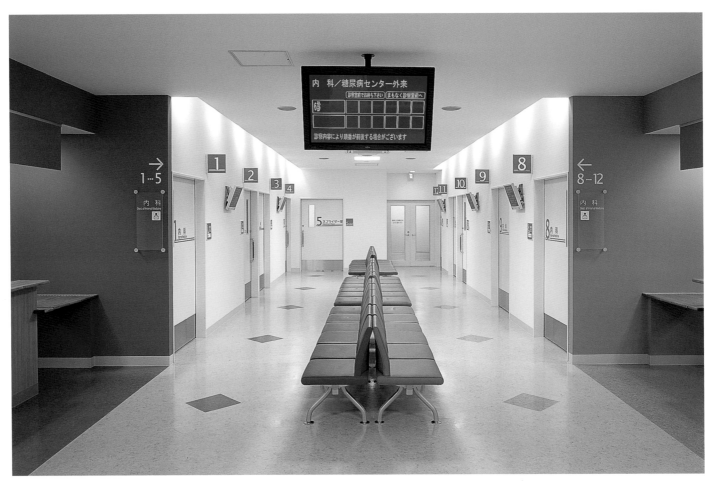

A calm green expressing the partnership with the Ebina General Hospital is the keynote in exterior and first floor signs. Guidance signage and information from the hospital are clustered near the entrance so as not to be missed by patients. The second and third floors have been divided into four zones with four different colors for each of the treatment areas. Organizing not only the notice board but the color of the walls and satellites makes the way to the treatment rooms bright and easy to understand.

外構サイン、1階サインは海老名総合病院との連携を表した落ち着いたグリーンが基調。案内サインや病院からのお知らせを入口近くに集中して配置し、患者の目に必ず留まるようにした。2、3階は診療科ごとに4色でカラーゾーニングを実施。表示板だけでなく壁やサテライトの色も揃えることで、診療所への明るくわかりやすい誘導の手助けとなった。

Tokyo Women's Medical University Hospital
東京女子医科大学病院　総合外来センター

Hospital　病院

CL: Tokyo Women's Medical University　東京女子医科大学
CO, SB: Kotobuki Corporation　コトブキ
AR: GKK Architects & Engineers　現代建築研究所
P(ss): Nacása & Partners　ナカサアンドパートナーズ

JAPAN　2003

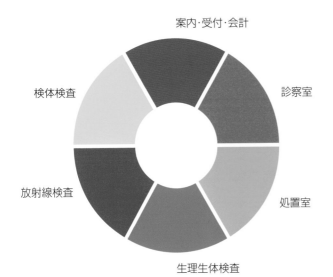

案内・受付・会計
診察室
処置室
生理生体検査
放射線検査
検体検査

Designed with a large atrium in the center to enable patients and visitors to easily grasp their current location. Signs use simple wording to provide essential information, clearly emphasizing different areas according to function, such as reception, examination, test, treatment and accounts areas, using color coding. Contrast was created using rich colors on signs in comparison to the subdued hues used in the architecture. Addresses, such as "Floor Number - Area - Room Number" are written in large letters on doors, blending colors to enable a simple wayfinding system.

自分の位置関係を把握できるよう大きなアトリウムを中心に設計。サインは言葉で簡単に表現ができ、違いがわかるよう、受付、診療、検査、処置、会計と機能別に色を分けた。色を抑えた建築に対して、サインは彩度の高い色を使うことでコントラストをつけた。扉には、住所のように "階-エリア-室番号" が大きく書かれ、色と合わせて簡単な案内を可能にした。

Koga Hospital 21　医療法人天神会　古賀病院21

Hospital　病院

CL: Medical Foundation Tenjinkai　医療法人天神会
DF, AR: Nikken Sekkei　日建設計
CO, SB: Kotobuki Corporation　コトブキ
P(ss): Tokuaki Takimoto　滝本徳明

JAPAN　2002

Not only signage but also theme colors reflected in the furniture and the color of the walls have been used on the floors. Lighting has been incorporated into the patient rooms and visibility has increased. Protruding signs have been utilized at complicated turning points where it is difficult to see ahead. Each of the general counters has been situated so as to protrude, making them easy to see even from a distance.

フロアにはサインだけでなく、家具や壁の色にまで反映したテーマカラーを設定。病室表示サインには照明が組み込まれ、視認性が高くなっている。また、見通しのきかない複雑な分岐点には突き出しサインを活用している。総合案内カウンターはそれぞれのカウンターが突き出した形に配置されているため、遠くからでもわかりやすいようになっている。

University of California, San Diego Cancer Center

Cancer Center 癌センター

CL: Rebecca & John Moores, University of California, San Diego Cancer Center
S: Charles Kaminski, Senior Architect, University of California, San Diego
PC, DD: Jeff Haack, The McCulley Group
D: Jeff Haack & Emily Phillips, The McCulleyu Group
DF, SB: The McCulley Group
Signage Construction: Karman Ltd.
General Building Contractor: McCarthy Building Cos. Inc.
AR: Zimmer Gunsul Frasca Partnership   P(ss): Kathy Mitome, The McCulley Group

USA 2005

The project aimed to develop an exterior and interior signage system that would follow the architectural vernacular, becoming a natural extension of the building design. Natural materials such as brushed aluminum and glass compliment the glass elements of the building, contrasting with a wood-shingled ceiling and vertical surfaces hosting one of forty vibrant colors. The package included etched glass panels illuminated with fiber optics commemorating those who contributed to the construction of the facility.

このプロジェクトでは建築の風合いに調和した屋内外のサインシステム構築が目指された。つや消しアルミや建物のガラス素材にあったガラスなど、サインのシンプルな材質が、板ばり天井や40色の鮮やかな色の1つが使われた壁面と対照をなしている。光ファイバー照射のエッチングが施されたガラスパネルは建設の功労者たちを記念したもの。

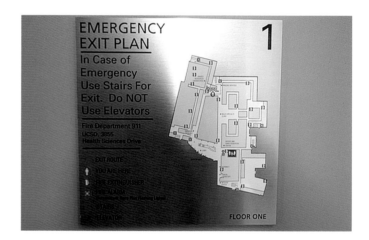

Main Hospital Lower Austria

Hospital 病院

CL: Government Lower Austria
PR: Schmied AG
PC: Monika Rosenkranz
DD: Erwin K. Bauer
D: Dieter Mayer
P: Gisela Erlacher
DF, CO, SB: Bauer-Concept & Design
AR: Pfaffenbichler

AUSTRIA 2006

Intuitive orientation for a new building in the hospital district of the capital of Lower Austria. The new system establishes a wording system for all institutions on the site, and with every department following the new system, ensures understandability for users without special medical knowledge. Good readability, the use of strong colors in combination with large arrows applied directly to walls, and new clear symbols for the infrastructure, add a significant note to the modern, open architecture.

下オーストリア州都の病院地域の新病棟のための直観的サインシステム。建物内の全施設に一貫した言語表現体系を構築したことで特殊な医療知識のない患者でもわかりやすい表示が実現。文字を見やすくしたり、目立つ色の大矢印を壁に直接描いたり、施設を明瞭なシンボルで表したサインは、モダンでオープンな建物の印象をさらに高めている。

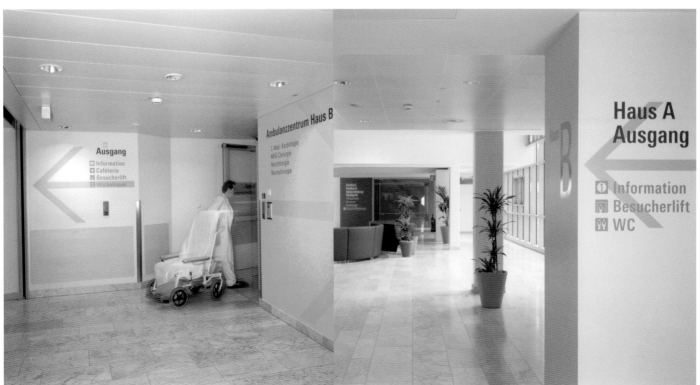

Juntendo University Urayasu Hospital

順天堂大学医学部附属 順天堂浦安病院

Hospital 病院

CL: Juntendo University Urayasu Hospital 順天堂大学医学部附属 順天堂浦安病院
S, AR: Shimizu Corporation 清水建設 設計本部
DF, CO, SB: Kotobuki Corporation コトブキ
P(ss): Tokuaki Takimoto 滝本徳明

JAPAN 2004

1F平面図

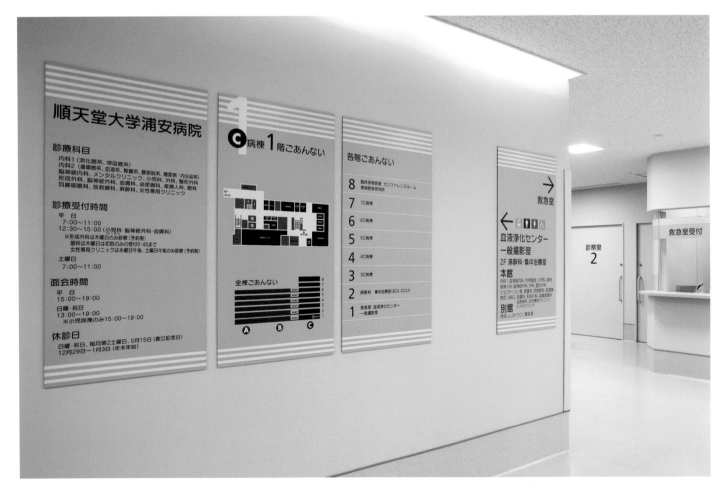

Signs created with pink as a base to promote an image of cheerfulness and health. Floor and wall surfaces are color coordinated with the signage, creating a warm, comforting atmosphere. Floor numbers are indicated in large characters below nurse-station counters. The goal of the signage programs was not only to provide critical information, but also to create an enjoyable and soothing atmosphere, as seen in the signs hung from the ceiling with their easy-to-read large lettering.

サインはピンクをベースにした明るく健康的なイメージ。床面や壁面もサインと同じカラーコーディネートのため、あたたかみのある和やかな雰囲気を演出。ナースステーションカウンターの下には大きく階数表示を入れ、天吊のサインは大きな文字で読みやすく設定するなど、サインとして正確で必要な役割を果たすだけでなく雰囲気を作ることを目指した。

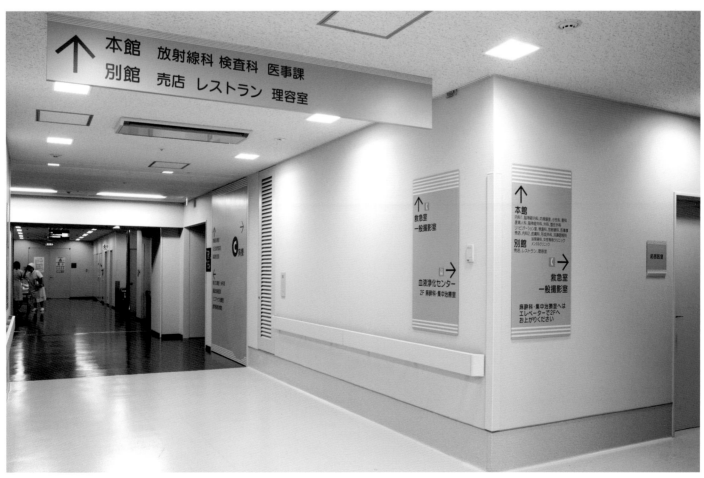

Thunder Bay Regional Health Sciences Center

Medical Center 医療センター

CL, AR: Faroow Partnership Architects
S: Wayne McCutcheon
Producer of Signage: Les Enseignes Perfection, Alain Dupuis
DD: Veronica Chan (Entro Communications)
D: Raymond Cheung, Gigi Lau, Jennifer Marshall
P, P(ss): Kerun IP
DF, SB: Entro Communications
CO: Ellis Don Construction, Tom Jones Corp.

CANADA 2004

The architectural design of the Thunder Bay Regional Health Sciences Centre infuses the complex with healing qualities linked to the environment. Clear navigation was important and emphasis was placed on integrating three different languages: English, French, and native Oji-Cree. The biggest challenge was how to communicate, with its multi-lingual treatment, in a way easily understood by patients, visitors, and staff members. The program included exterior and interior identity and wayfinding signage and building identification.

サンダーベイ地域健康科学センターの設計では環境と調和した癒し効果が目指され、案内表示をわかりやすくすることが特に重要となった。最も難題は、英語、フランス語、先住民のオジ・クリー語の3言語を患者、訪問客、職員にいかに理解しやすく表示するかであった。このプロジェクトでは屋内外に道案内や建物の案内などが設置された。

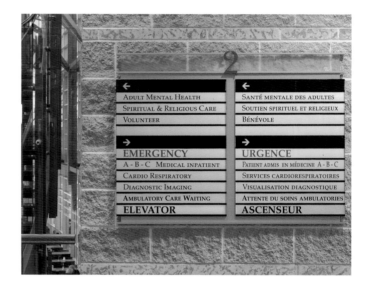

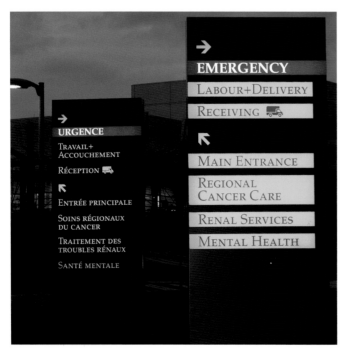

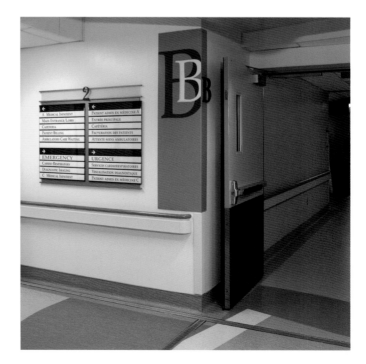

Staples Corporate Headquarters

Office Products Manufacturer 事務機器メーカー

CL: Staples Corporation
DD: Clifford Selbert
D: Greg Welch, Patrick Gray
DF, SB: Selbert Perkins Design
P(ss): Anton Grassl

USA 2002

Environmental graphics and wayfinding for the interior of the corporate headquarters building of Staples Corporation, the number one office supply superstore company in the United States.

アメリカ最大規模のオフィス用品店を展開するステープルズ・コーポレーションの本社内の環境グラフィックスとサイン。

Floor Guide

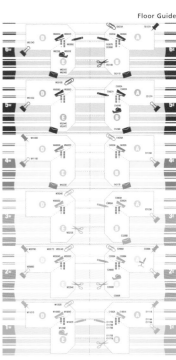

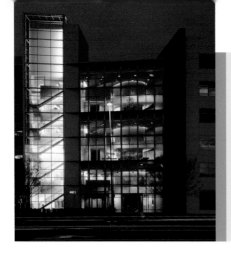

Nortel Santa Clara Optical Switching Enterprise

Global Communications　コンピュータ会社

CL: Nortel Networks
S: Jonathan Corey
PC: Ed Stanyk
DD: Hal Kantner
D: Craig Hein, Mark Askew, Diana Gonzalez
P: Hal Kantner, Craig Hein
DF: Hok San Francisco　CO: Vision 20/20
Project Designer: Matthew Winkelstein　SB: Hok Visual Communications

USA　2003

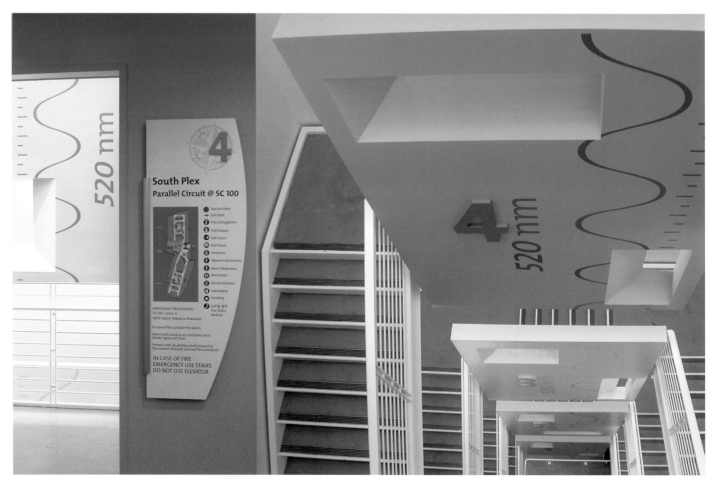

A six-story facility supporting the evolving use of light waves to transport data and knowledge, hence the theme "light makes vision possible" and references to the physics of light and color. Each of the six floors was presented in a dominant wavelength of the visible light spectrum, with higher wavelengths on higher floors. The primary color code of a floor drives the palette for graphics and quotes on that floor. Black, white, and gray are used for the graphics and signage that repeat on all six floors.

6階建ての建物にデータと知識を伝播する光の波が展開。「光がビジョンを実現する」というテーマを光と色で表現している。上階ほど波長が高くなる可視光スペクトルの波で各階がおおわれている。各階固有のグラフィックスにはその階の基調色から派生した色が、全階に共通するグラフィックスとサインには黒、白、グレイが使われている。

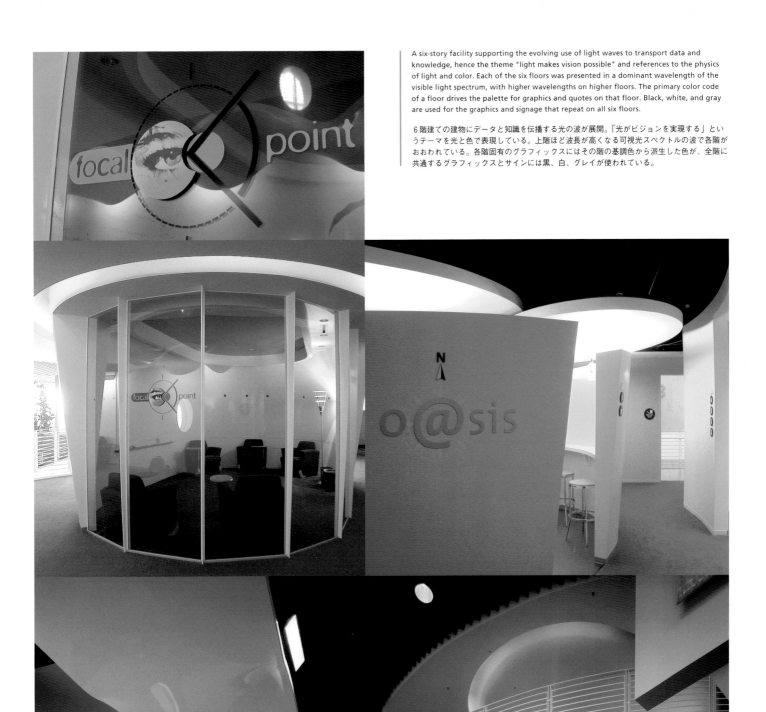

London Stock Exchange

Financial　金融

CL: London Stock Exchange
PC, D: Evelyn Fujimoto
P: Marcus Peel & Tim Soar
DF, SB: Gensler
AR: Eric Parry Architects

UK　2004

The design approach adopted a fresh perspective: to be radical while being sympathetic to the company's history and its exiting surroundings. The graphics mirror and enhance a fascinating interior that is both inspiring to walk around and to work in. The project was a unique opportunity to rejuvenate the workplace and improve the work habits of one of the most influential financial institutions in the world.

「ラディカルでありながら証券所の歴史と既存の環境に調和するもの」という斬新な視点をデザインに採用。内装を反映したグラフィックスは、歩き回るにも仕事をするにも人をやる気にさせる内装の魅力をさらに高めている。本プロジェクトは世界で最も大きな影響力を持つ金融機関のオフィスを活性化し、作業慣行を改善するまたとない機会となった。

Natura

Cosmetic 化粧品メーカー

CL: Natura
S: Marisa Caldas
PR: Luiz Eduardo Graziano
PC, DD: André Poppovic
D: Angela Winter, Carolina Olsson, Luciana Turco, Vilmar Pellisson, Lúcio Luz
DF, SB: Oz Design
CO: Koike Arquitetura da Imagem
P(ss): Eduardo Moraes

BRAZIL 2004

This signage program created a universe of more than a thousand signs located throughout the 14 buildings of the industrial complex.

このサインプロジェクトでは1,000点以上のサインが制作され、敷地内にある14棟の施設全体に設置された。

Crate&Barrel World Headquarters

Housewares 家庭用品メーカー

CL: Crate&Barrel Inc.
D: Chris Calori, Principal in Charge, David Vanden-Eynden, Adrisory Principal, Denise Funaro, Designer
AR: Perkins & Will, Architects
SB: Calori & Vanden-Eynden

USA 2002

The signage program for C&B's new world headquarters promotes the company's brand image. Monumental cubes identify the site; clean lines, simple forms and black on white typography while subtle background images echo the architecture and the nature of the C&B design aesthetic – playful yet restrained. The interior sign program includes a zone numbering and orientation system that allows for future expansion while taking into account the realities of data and emergency communications information.

ブランドイメージ向上を図った、C&B社の新世界本社のサイン。モニュメント型の直方体がVIの中心。シンプルな線と形、薄色で図柄を入れたの白地に黒のタイポグラフィは建物と同社のデザイン美学「抑制のきいた陽気さ」を反映。屋内はゾーンごとに番号がふられ、将来の増築に対応したサインシステムも導入。正確な情報表示や緊急時連絡も考慮されている。

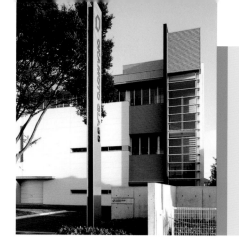

Okamoto Glass Co., Ltd. Thin Film Factory
岡本硝子薄膜事業所

Glass　硝子メーカー

CL: Okamoto Glass Co., Ltd.　岡本硝子
PR: Koji Yoneda　米田浩二　PC: Shinya Takemoto　武本真哉
DD, D: Kazunari Suzuki　鈴木一成　DF, SB: Ilya Corporation　イリア
CO: Kajima Corporation　鹿島建設　AR: Kajima Design　KAJIMA DESIGN
P(ss): Nozomu Shimao, Hiroshi Tsujitani　島尾 望 辻谷 宏

JAPAN 2003

The thin film operation of firm Okamoto Glass develops and manufactures heat-permeable, heat-diffusing light-reflecting glass products such as car headlights and dental mirrors. In the signage plan, the factory was seen as a place to project the company's corporate identity, and simple, clear signs created, with a glass motif. The result is a pleasant workspace for the factory's employees.

岡本硝子薄膜事業所は、プロジェクターや自動車のヘッドライト、デンタルミラーなど、熱を透過・拡散させながら光反射する硝子製品を開発・製造している。サイン計画では、工場をコーポレート・アイデンティティの発信の場としてとらえ、ガラスをモチーフにしたシンプルで明快なサインを実現。従業員が快適に働ける空間を作りあげている。

Nortel Billerica Executive Briefing Center

Global Communications　コンピュータ会社

CL: Nortel Networks
S: Tom Lynch, Mike Phelan
PC: Aditya Mahajan, David Kusturin
DD: Hal Kantner
D: Mark Askew, Craig Hein, Jeff Erlich, Diana Gonzalez
P: Hal Kantner, Craig Hein　DF: HOK
CO: Vision Factory, Vision Zolzo　AR: Hok DC, Billhellmuth-Principal Designer
SB: Hok Visual Communications

USA　2003

This state of the art facility was built around the client's brand attributes and visualized their position statement, "How the World Shares Ideas", by making extensive use of digital output to create custom murals printed on various media. Fabric, furniture, and finishes were also used to project the attributes "global" and "creative". The meeting rooms were named "How", "World", "Shares", and "Ideas". Monitor displays and media content were balanced with traditional graphics such as 3D letters on custom furniture.

依頼主のブランド属性を核に建設された最先端のビル。様々な素材にデジタル出力で印刷された壁画が企業テーマ「How the World Shares Ideas（世界はどのように知識を共有するか）」を視覚化。布、家具、仕上げ塗料が属性の「グローバル」「創造性」を表現。会議室名は「How」「World」「Shares」「Ideas」に。モニター表示や壁画は既存デザインとの調和も考慮された。

Chugoku Shimbun Hiroshima Press Center
中国新聞広島制作センター"ちゅーピーパーク"

Press Center　新聞社制作センター

CL: The Chugoku Shimbun　中国新聞社
PR: Koji Yoneda　米田浩二　PC: Hiroyuki Togo　東郷裕幸
DD: Kazunari Suzuki　鈴木一成　D: Yukiko Nakashima　中島由記子
DF, SB: Ilya Corporation　イリア　Furniture Design: Dentsu Inc.　電通
CO: Kajima Corporation　鹿島建設
AR: Kajima Design　KAJIMA DESIGN　P(ss): Masayori Yano　矢野勝偉

JAPAN　2005

A newspaper printworks erected in one corner of a neighborhood leisure center designed as a place for readers and local residents to meet and socialize. The concept is that of a printworks in the middle of a forest, and the complex includes an open plaza in attractive natural surroundings and a multipurpose hall. Cartoon characters, a round motif resembling a roll of newsprint, and woodgrain pattern were incorporated in the signage, the aim being to design fun signs appealing to visitors of all ages.

読者と地域住民の交流拠点として、地元レジャー施設の一角に建てられた新聞印刷工場。森の中の工場をテーマに、自然に囲まれたふれあい広場や、多目的ホールが併設されている。サイン計画では、イメージキャラクターや巻き取り紙をイメージした円形モチーフ、木目調パターンなどを取り入れ、来場者の幅広い年齢層に対応した楽しいサインを目指した。

食 堂

廃インキ
処理室

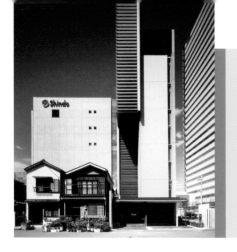

Shindo Company Ltd. Ryogoku Head Office
新藤両国本社ビル

Printing　印刷会社

CL: Tokyo Hozen Co., Ltd.　東京保全
PR: Koji Yoneda　米田浩二　PC: Hiroyuki Togo　東郷裕幸
DD: Kazunari Suzuki　鈴木一成　D: Yukiko Nakashima　中島由記子
DF, SB: Ilya Corporation　イリア　CO: Kajima Corporation　鹿島建設
AR: Kajima Design　KAJIMA DESIGN　P(ss): Nozomu Shimao　島尾 望

JAPAN　2004

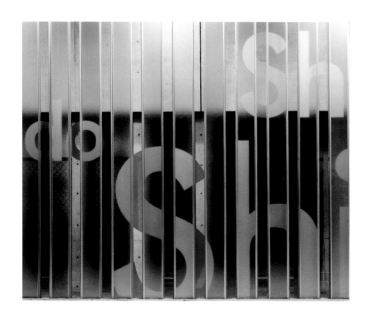

Signage plan for the head office and plant of Shindo fine art printers. The aim was to express the company's philosophy and ensure a good fit with the surrounding environment, at the same time making best use of the atmosphere of the working-class neighborhood of Ryogoku, cradle of Edo culture. All signage features monotone shades and grid dots inspired by the unique interplay of light and shade in the area, maroon coloring to convey a sense of Edo culture and tradition, and the Shindo logo graphic integrated into the architecture.

高級美術印刷を手がける新藤の本社と工場のサイン計画。江戸文化発祥の地である両国の下町の風情を生かしながら、企業理念の表現と周辺環境との調和を目指した。サインは下町独特の光と影の空間を意識したモノトーンの色彩と格子状ドット、江戸の文化と伝統を感じさせる海老茶色、建築と一体化したShindoロゴのグラフィックでまとめた。

© Yukio Shimizu

Shiodome Tower 汐留タワー

Office Building オフィスビルディング

CL: Kajima Shiodome Kaihatsu Co., Ltd. 鹿島汐留開発
PR: Koichi Ando (Ando Gallery, Inc.) 安東孝一（アンドーギャラリー）
DD: Hiroshi Egawa (Kajima Design) 江川 博（KAJIMA DESIGN）
D: Kaoru Kasai (Sun-Ad Company Limited) 葛西 薫（サン・アド）
CO: From To Inc. フロムトゥ
AR: Kajima Design, Mitsubishi Jisho Sekkei Inc. KAJIMA DESIGN 三菱地所設計
SB: Kajima Corporation 鹿島建設

JAPAN 2003

Shiodome Tower created in the image of an elegant body. Signage was regarded as accessories with which to decorate the body. The aim was to create warmth, not chills; to exude charm, not perfection; and to bring about a nostalgic future, not an overly digitized world.

SHIODOME TOWERはエレガントな肉体である。研ぎすまされた品格を備えながら、その肌から豊かな香りを放っている。SHIODOME TOWERに施されたサインは、いわばその身につけるアクセサリーとなる。冷たさではなく温かさ　潔べきではなく色香　超デジタルではなくノスタルジックな未来……　肌色のスーツに真っ赤なアクセサリー。原石が磨かれて宝石となったように、鉱物が硬いのに柔らかいように。

Oita Canon Inc.　大分キヤノン大分事業所

Factory　工場

CL: Canon Inc.　キヤノン
PR: Yoshifumi Matsumoto　松本好史
PC: Tadashi Fujimura　藤村 正
DD: Takahiro Yamada　山田隆宏
D: Kazunari Suzuki, Yukiko Nakashima　鈴木一成　中島由記子
P, P(ss): Shinsuke Kera　解良信介
DF: Kajima Design, Ilya Corporation　鹿島建設 設計本部 イリア
CO: Kajima Kyushu Branch　鹿島九州支店　SB: Kajima Design　鹿島建設 設計本部
JAPAN 2005

Plant engaged in the production of digital camera components, camera assembly and distribution. A complex of several buildings, each with a different function centered on the manufacturing operation, is situated in leafy surroundings. Concepts for the signage were "pleasant, safe, and expression of the company's business philosophy". Using stripes as a base in a reference to Canon's advanced capabilities and sense of speed, traditional Japanese colors were employed in easy to understand signs with an emphasis on achieving a coordinated look across all buildings.

デジタルカメラの部品製造、組立、製品物流の一貫工場。建物は生産部門を中心に、機能別の建築物数棟が緑豊かな自然の中に配置されている。サイン計画は快適、安全、企業姿勢の表現がコンセプト。キヤノンが持つ先進性やスピード感を表現するストライプを基調に、日本の伝統色を配し、建築空間との一体感を重視したわかりやすいサインを実現した。

Sacos Mother Factory　サコスマザーファクトリー

Heavy Construction Equipment Lease Company　建設重機リース会社

CL: Sacos　サコス
DF, SB: Archi+Air, Wataru Nishei, Kiyohisa Furuya　アーキエア　二瓶 渉　古谷清寿
CO: Ohara Archi & Builders　大原工務所
P(ss): Hiroshi Ueda　上田 宏

JAPAN 2004

Renewal of the materials warehouse coincided with the establishment of factory expansion at a new destination for this heavy construction equipment lease company. It seemed impossible to introduce new signage consisting of simple objects into a huge, 104.0m x 25.0m space, so the program aimed at using the actual architecture - the walls, floors and doors - as signs, resulting in a keen awareness of the space around oneself. The architecture itself became the visual identity of the signage.

建設重機リース会社の工場拡張にともない移転先である資材倉庫をリニューアルすることとなった。新たにサインを単体のオブジェとして挿入する方法では104.0m×25.0mの巨大な空間にはどんな作用も働かないのではと考え、建築の部位である壁、床、扉にサインを同化させることによって、空間そのものを意識させようと思った。建築そのものがVIとなっている。

Mitsui Oil Self SS　三井石油セルフSS

Oil Marketing　石油販売

CL: Mitsui Oil Marketing Support Co., Ltd.　三井石油販売
PR: Yasunobu Johno　城野康信
PC: Nobuaki Yuasa　湯浅信昭
DD: Gaku Ohta　太田 岳
D: Gaku Ohta, Toshihiko Morita　太田 岳　森田利彦
DF, SB: Nippon Design Center　日本デザインセンター

JAPAN 2002

A new brand-mark expressing the Mitsui Oil Co. corporate stance of working in harmony with the global environment. The green background color of service stations was selected to encourage drivers to want to stop by and check out the station, providing an Oasis environment for those on the road. Pylon signs also display the emblematic brand-mark, creating an image of the green fields of the earth and bright dreams fulfilled.

新しいブランドマークは、地球環境との調和を考える三井石油の企業姿勢を表現。グリーンを基調とするSSのカラーリングは、「寄ってみたくなるSS」を目指し、ロードビジネスの「オアシス」としての環境を提供する。パイロンサインに象徴されるブランドマークは、緑の大地、明るい夢のふくらみをイメージさせる。

Parking Diamant

Property Developer　資産運用会社

CL: Diamant Building (Brussels)
S, PC, DD: Chantal Veys
PR, DF, CO, SB: ÉO Design Partners s.a.
D: Alasdair Grant
P(ss): Yvan Glavie

BELGIUM 2001

Pedestrian wayfinding in a one-story underground car park with two zones: North, featuring a warmly dressed figure walking against the wind and the cool color blue, and South, a lightly dressed figure walking effortlessly and the warm color ochre. The volume of color used on each sign increases as the signs approach the door. The walking silhouettes indicate the direction to the door, painted directly on the concrete walls, with letters and arrows applied thereafter.

2ゾーンに区分された、1階のみの地下駐車場の歩行者案内。北ゾーンでは暖かく服を着込んだ人物が風に向かって歩く図に寒色の青が、南ゾーンでは軽装の人物が軽やかに歩く図に黄土色が使われている。各サインの彩色領域はドアに近づくほど拡大。歩く人物の影絵はみなドアに向かっている。コンクリート壁に直接描かれた図のうえに文字と矢印が加えられた。

Bank Boston

Bank 銀行

CL: Bank Boston
S: Arquiteto Renato Kaufmann
PR: Buzas e Buzas
PC, DD, D, AR: Rogerio Batagliesi, Antonio Malicia
P, P(ss): Marcos Muzzi
DF, SB: Batagliesi e Associados Limitada

BRAZIL 2002

The design worked with and played off of a number of planes and curves present in the building's formal language, as well as giving a sculptural, three dimensional character to all the signing elements.

建物に多用され、設計要素である平面や曲線と調和し、これらをさらに美しく演出している デザインは、すべてのサインエレメントに彫刻のような立体感を与えている。

Ciel Grand Narita　シエールグラン成田

Employee Dormitory　社員寮

CL: Japan Airport Terminal Co.,Ltd.　日本空港ビルデング
PC, AR: Mitsubishi Jisho Sekkei Inc. Residential Design & Engineering Department　三菱地所 住宅設計部
DD: Isamu Sugeno (Mitsubishi Jisho Sekke Inc. Residential Design & Engineering Department)
菅野 勇（三菱地所 住宅設計部）
D: Miyuki Kameya　亀谷美幸
CO: Hirose & Co., Ltd.　ヒロセ
P: Kenjiro Yoshimi (Studio Bauhaus) and others　吉見謙次郎（スタジオバウハウス）他
SB: Enviro-System Inc.　エンバイロ・システム

JAPAN 2004

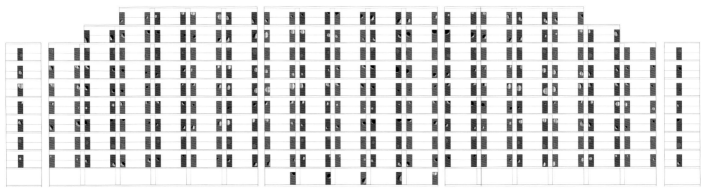

全体図

Company housing for JAL employees and associates. An attempt was made to give the long, sterile rows of 630 apartment doors facing onto a courtyard a more expressive, human face. The JAL corporate colors of red, black and silver were employed in a moon design for the east block, and sun for the west, using the doors of each apartment to convey the impression of the sun and moon moving slowly around the courtyard.

JALの社員と関係者のための集合住宅。中庭に面してズラリと並んだ全630室の無機質なドアの列を、人間的な表情豊かなものにしようと試みた。JALのコーポレートカラーである赤・黒・銀を用い、E棟は月、W棟は太陽を表現。一室一室のドアを月と太陽がゆっくりと中庭を巡っていくようにイメージした。

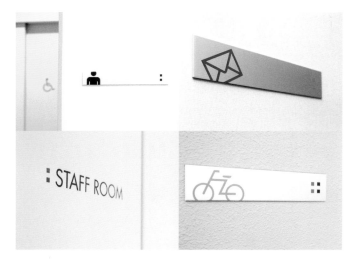

Canon Yufuin Asagiri-kan　キヤノン湯布院あさぎり館

Sanatorium　保養所

CL: Canon　キヤノン
S: Akio Kurosaka (Kajima Design Kyushu)　黒坂章雄（KAJIMA DESIGN Kyushu）
PR: Norio Fuchigami (Kajima Design Kyushu)　渕上紀生（KAJIMA DESIGN Kyushu）
PC, AR: Shin Takano (Kajima Design Kyushu)　高野 信（KAJIMA DESIGN Kyushu）
DD, CO: Toshihiro Yamamoto (Hadakogeisha)　山本俊祐（ハダ工芸社）
D, P, P(ss): Hitomi Ishikawa (Hadakogeisha)　石川ひとみ（ハダ工芸社）
SB: Hadakogeisha　ハダ工芸社

JAPAN 2002

Sanatorium built in the mountains of Yufuin, in the scenic hot springs area popular throughout Japan. The name "Morning Mist Building" comes from the fact that Yufuin is famous for its morning mists. The main concept was "signage that reflects new qualities of Japanese-style design". A special handcrafted finish for the copper used as the base material, and materials and color schemes which fuse with the scenery of Yufuin were considered in the scheme.

全国的に人気の高い風情豊かな温泉地、湯布院の山間に建てられた保養施設。「あさぎり館」の名は湯布院が朝霧でも有名なことにちなむ。サインデザインのメインコンセプトは「和風の中にもどこか新しさを感じるサインデザイン」。ベースの素材に銅を用い、特殊な手作業で仕上げを施すなど、湯布院の風景に溶け込むような素材や色調を考慮した。

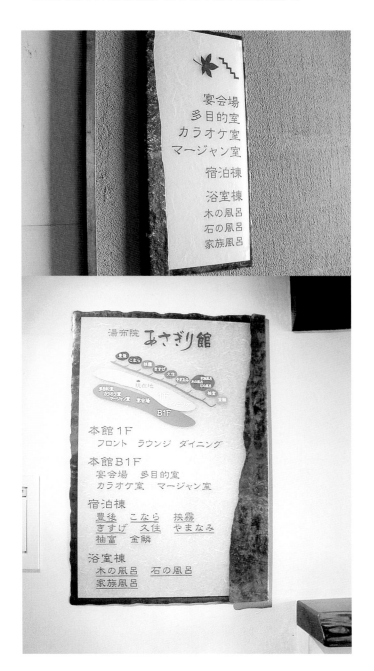

Contemporary Art Museum, Kumamoto
熊本市現代美術館

Museum 美術館

CL: Kumamoto Kamitouri District A Municipal Redevelopment Consortium 熊本市上通A地区市街地再開発組合
DF, AR: Azusa Sekkei Co., Ltd. 梓設計
CO, SB: Kotobuki Corporation コトブキ
P(ss): Tokuaki Takimoto 滝本徳明

JAPAN 2002

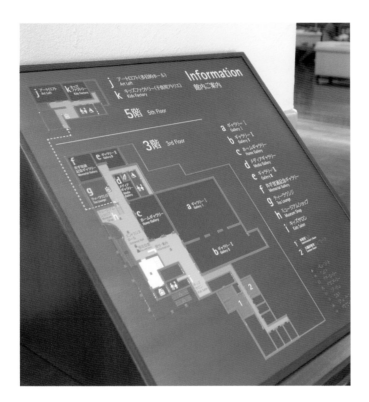

The pictographs appearing as handwritten works give the impression of an at-home atmosphere. The hard base of the signs was suppressed to bring out the warm feeling the wood material adds, and colorful felt, created by participants of a museum art program, was added to the pictograms. The yellow copper plates bring a subdued impression to the signs, a sort of friendly sophistication.

手書き風のオリジナルピクトは素朴な印象を与えている。基盤の色を抑え、木の暖かい雰囲気を損なわないよう配慮しつつ、ピクトグラムにはカラフルなフェルトを添えた。これらのフェルトは美術館のプログラムで参加者が作ったもの。また、黄銅版のサインは落ち着いた印象を与え、親しみやすい品格を感じさせている。

Baroque Castles and Historical Gardens of the Belvedere

Castles & Museum 教会 / ミュージアム

CL: Belvedere
PR: Metallbautreiber GesmbH
PC: Monika Rosenkranz
DD, D: Erwin K. Bauer
P: Lisa Mathis
DF, SB: Bauer-Concept & Design   CO, AR: Frank

AUSTRIA 2002

Interior and exterior wayfinding system designed to guide international cultural tourists through one of Austria's main sightseeing areas. The visual language with black and white text and symbols harmonizes with the historical ensemble, while lending it a modern touch. The system follows one design principle: It stands out because it doesn't stand out, but is available at every point where guidance is needed for orientation.

オーストリアの観光名所の屋内外に設置された案内システムが、海外から文化の探訪に訪れたツーリストをガイド。白と黒の文字や記号を使った視覚言語は歴史的建造物に調和すると同時にモダンな趣向も加えている。このシステムは「抑制した表現によって目を引く。また位置確認が必要な地点には必ず案内を設置」という設計原則に基づいている。

Ran Heritage Centre

Heritage Center 歴史博物館

CL: Royal Australian Navy
PC: Romaine Teahan
DD: Steven Joseph
D: Nicky Hardcastle
DF, P(ss), SB: Spatchurst
AR: Tompkins Mda

AUSTRALIA 2005

The visitor experience includes not only the Heritage Centre and Boatshed exhibitions, but many naval items on display on the grounds. Visitor access to the Centre is by ferry only, and the signage directs visitors to, and around, the Centre and it's grounds. The exhibition, exhibition graphics and directional signage were designed in tandem, thus the signage is part of a total design approach. It has a clean, contemporary look within the context of, and referencing, Australian naval heritage while conforming to Brand Navy guidelines.

ヘリテージ・センターや艇庫の展示と、海軍にまつわる多数の展示を鑑賞できる施設への交通手段は、フェリーだけ。展示品や、展示品をあしらったグラフィックスに並べられた案内標示は建物や周辺をガイドしながらもデザイン全体に溶け込み、ブランド・ネービーのガイドラインに沿いつつ、オーストラリア海軍の遺産をすっきりと現代的に演出。

Kitakyushu Museum of Natural History and Human History 北九州市立自然史・歴史博物館

Museum 博物館

CL: Kitakyushu City 北九州市
DD: Taro Watanabe (Emotional Space Design Inc.) 渡辺太郎（エモーショナル・スペース・デザイン）
D: Yoko Hayakawa (Emotional Space Design Inc.) 早川容子（エモーショナル・スペース・デザイン）
P, SB: Emotional Space Design Inc. エモーショナル・スペース・デザイン
CO: Kotobuki Corporation コトブキ
AR, Design Partner: Kume Sekkei 久米設計

JAPAN 2003

The signage system here, acting as the "index" or directory for a building design concept consisting of "an indexing plan for the museum complex", is designed to give clear directions to each of the museum's accessible spaces. A fixed point sign system made from lightproof mesh sheets in different theme colors was installed on the borders between spaces, and consists of signs suspended from the ceiling, clearly marking each display area.

設計コンセプト「ミュージアム・コンプレックスのインデックス計画」の"インデックス"の役割を担ったサイン計画は、開かれたいろいろな空間へ、明確に導くことができるよう配慮。各展示空間の境目にテーマカラーごとの遮光性メッシュシートによる定点サインシステムを導入。天井から吊り下げられた各展示エリアが明確にわかるようなシステムになっている。

Kawagoe City Art Museum　川越市立美術館

Museum　美術館

CL: Kawagoe City　川越市
DD: Taro Watanabe (Emotional Space Design Inc.)　渡辺太郎（エモーショナル・スペース・デザイン）
D: Yoko Hayakawa (Emotional Space Design Inc.)　早川容子（エモーショナル・スペース・デザイン）
P, SB: Emotional Space Design Inc.　エモーショナル・スペース・デザイン
CO: Kotobuki Corporation　コトブキ
S, AR: Sakakura Associates　坂倉建築研究所

JAPAN 2003

In matching the atmosphere of the museum, thick cutouts of guide maps and exhibition room names are used to bring out a subdued accent on the signage. Kawagoe is often called Little Edo, and still maintains many signs of its history as Japan's foremost post station. Even the museum itself, with its whitewash walls and tiled roof, is full of elements radiating the feeling of "wa" or harmony. The map graphics integrate those elements of "wa" in a form called "lattice work graphics", aiming at signage with a rather modern Japanese look.

施設空間との調和をはかって、カットアウトした案内マップや展示室名の切文字には厚みを持たせ、さりげなく空間のアクセントとなるようにした。川越は小江戸と呼ばれ、昔ながらの日本の宿場町としての面影を数多く残している。この美術館にも白い壁に瓦屋根など随所に和を感じさせる要素が取り入れられているが、マップグラフィックにはその和の要素を格子というかたちで取り入れ、現代の和の表現を目指した。

The National Science Museum · New Building
国立科学博物館・新館

Science Museum　科学博物館

CL: The National Science Museum　国立科学博物館　Design Direction: Tanseisha and Nomura Design JV, Hiroshi Inagaki 丹青社・乃村工藝社設計共同体　稲垣 博　Display Direction: Tanseisha and Nomura Design JV, Hisaya Takahashi　丹青社・乃村工藝社設計共同体　高橋久弥　Contents Graphic Direction: Tanseisha and Nomura Design JV, Koji Otsuka, Takashi Sato 丹青社・乃村工藝社設計共同体　大塚孝二　佐藤 尚　Sign Direction: Tanseisha and Nomura Design JV, Kazuko Kawasaki　丹青社・乃村工藝社設計共同体　川崎和子　Sign Design: Tanseisha and Nomura Design JV, Kazuko Kawasaki, Kuniyoshi Ono 丹青社・乃村工藝社設計共同体　川崎和子　小野邦理　P: Setsuo Hirosaki　廣崎節雄　DF: Tanseisha and Nomura Design JV　丹青社・乃村工藝社設計共同体　Construction: Nomura and Tanseisha Construction JV　乃村工藝社・丹青社展示工事共同企業体 CO: 丹青シグネクス　ノムラコムス　AR: Y.Ashihara Architect&Associates　芦原建築設計研究所　P(ss): Masami Daito　大東正巳　SB: Nomura Coms Co., Ltd. (Kuniyoshi Ono)　ノムラコムス（小野邦理）　　JAPAN 2004

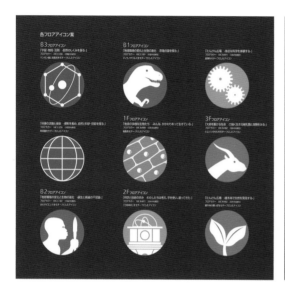

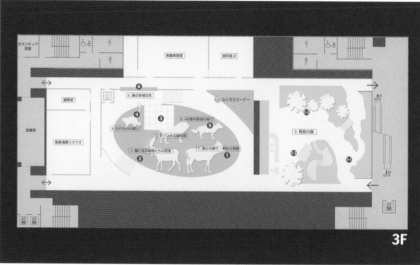

To make searching for information outside the museum simpler, street numbers were displayed on the exhibits and a standardized graphical expression and symbols used. The signage, being black, gave a sense of presence, the light spectrum was turned into a visual element and after interlocking the floor icons and maps, colors took into account visually impaired persons. Maps were expressed as graphics conveying an idea of the content of the exhibits.

国立科学博物館・新館は展示に番地を表示し統一的なグラフィックと表記システムでウエブ等館外からでも情報の検索や入手を容易にしている。サインは黒で存在感を出し、光のスペクトルをビジュアルエレメントとし、フロアアイコン、マップはそれと連動した上で色覚障害に配慮した色彩とした。またマップは展示内容を伝えるグラフィック表現とした。

Kure Maritime Museum (Yamato Museum)
呉市海事歴史科学館（大和ミュージアム）

Museum　科学館

CL: Kure City　呉市
DD: Taro Watanabe (Emotional Space Design Inc.)　渡辺太郎（エモーショナル・スペース・デザイン）
D: Ai Takaaki (Emotional Space Design Inc.)　高明 愛（エモーショナル・スペース・デザイン）
P, SB: Emotional Space Design Inc.　エモーショナル・スペース・デザイン
CO: Kotobuki Corporation　コトブキ
AR, Design Partner: Kume Sekkei　久米設計

JAPAN 2005

The Kure Maritime Museum (Yamato Museum) presents the history of science and technology in the city of Kure from pre-war times. Kure is known for its high-precision steelmaking technology, and this was reflected in the signage, which used contemporary modeling techniques to highlight the city's shipbuilding heritage. An example bending steel plate in the complex manner used in ship-building, and combining this with transparent glasswork inspired by the Kure coast.

呉市海事歴史科学館（大和ミュージアム）は戦前と戦後を通して呉市の科学技術を紹介する施設。サイン計画では、呉のアイデンティティである高精度な製鋼技術の表現がテーマ。複雑な造船の曲げ加工を表現した鋼板に、呉の海をイメージした透明ガラスを合わせてデザイン処理を施すなど、呉の造船技術の歴史を現代的な造形表現手法で表した。

900 Jahre Zukunft

Cultural Center 文化施設

CL: Land Vorarlberg
PC, DD: Sandro Scherling+Sigi Ramoser
D: Sandro Scherling+Sigi Ramoser, Stefan Gassner, Michael Mittermayer
P: Sepp Führer
DF: Sägenvier Designkommunikation
AR: Ernst Giselbrecht
SB: Sigi Ramoser

AUSTRIA 1999

"900 years future" was the title of an exhibition held in an historic Catholic cloister that explores as its theme the future of human life. The concept is represented in visually in the event graphics design by a flying monastery and an astronaut. A red boardwalk guides the visitor through the cloister, from the entrance wall to the sea. The floor guide shows the different time-rooms and guides visitors through the exhibition.

「900年、未来」はカトリックの歴史的修道院で開催された、人の生命の未来を探求するというテーマの展覧会のタイトル。そのコンセプトは空飛ぶ修道院や宇宙飛行士のイベントグラフィックスで視覚的に表現された。赤い板張りの道がゲストを入口の壁から海まで修道院全体を案内。フロアガイドが様々な時代の部屋を示し、展覧会全体をガイド。

Tokyo Big Sight　東京ビッグサイト

Convention Center　コンベンションセンター

CL: Tokyo Big Sight Inc.　東京ビッグサイト
DD: Yasuo Katakura (Rei Design & Plannings)　片倉保夫（黎デザイン総合計画研究所）
D: Hirofumi Shinohara, Dan Tamura (Rei Design & Plannings)　篠原博文　田村 弾（黎デザイン総合計画研究所）
P: Shinichi Tomita　富田眞一
CO: From To Inc.　フロムトゥ
SB: Rei Design & Plannings　黎デザイン総合計画研究所

JAPAN 2004

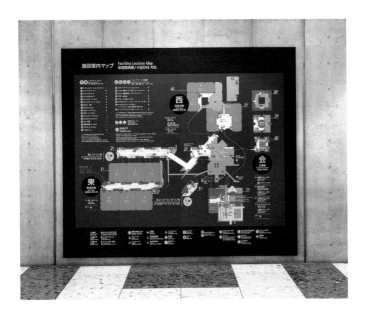

Reconstruction planning for the signage of Tokyo Big Sight. The concept was to convert, by using information, the super-scale structures built in the Bubble period into comfortable and relaxing places for ordinary people to use successfully. Implemented over the course of two years, by relocating the signage the program focused on reidentifying spaces, distinguishing traffic paths, color coding zones, and making map expressions clear.

東京ビッグサイト案内サイン改善計画のコンセプトは、バブル期に建てられたスーパースケールの構造物を、人々が円滑に使いこなせるように、また息長く使えるように、情報によって再構築することであった。サインの再配置による空間見通しの確保、動線の明確化、色彩コードの徹底、地図表現の明瞭化などのテーマに知恵を絞った。なおこの見直しの検討には、2か年の歳月を費やしている。

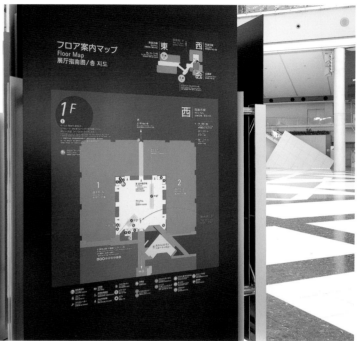

Pacifico Yokohama Exhibition Hall
パシフィコ横浜展示ホール

Convention Center　コンベンションセンター

CL: Pacific Convention Plaza Yokohama / Yokohama City Port and Harbor Bureau　横浜国際平和会議場 / 横浜市港湾局
AR, S: Nikken Sekkei　日建設計
DF, CO, SB: Kotobuki Corporation　コトブキ
P(ss): Nacása & Partners　ナカサアンドパートナーズ

JAPAN　2001

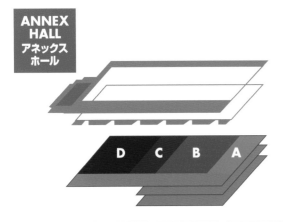

A complex convention center of a scale and grade rivaled by few throughout the world, opened in 1991 as the leading project in the new waterfront "Minato Mira 21 District," in the cosmopolitan city of Yokohama. Signage was redesigned for the renewal. The new signage employs the surfaces of the emergency doors as well as large banners, creating great eye-catchers. While maintaining strong presence within the interior, the banners create a rather airy and light mood.

国際都市横浜の新しいウォーターフロント「みなとみらい21地区」のリーディングプロジェクトとして平成3年にオープンした世界有数の規模とグレードを誇る複合型コンベンション施設。リニューアルにあわせて展示場内のサインを一新。壁面の防火扉を活用し空間に突出したアイキャッチとなるサインをバナータイプに変更。そのため目にとまる存在感を持ちながらも軽快な印象を与えている。

The 2005 World Exposition, Aichi, Japan
2005年日本国際博覧会

World Exposition 国際博覧会

CL: Japan Association For The 2005 World Exposition 財団法人2005年日本国際博覧会協会
DD: Kazuo Tanaka (GK Sekkei Inc.), Yasuo Yokota (GK Graphics Inc.) 田中一雄（GK設計）　横田保生（GKグラフィックス）
D: Kanji Kato ,Toshihiko Irie, Masako Nishikata (GK Sekkei Inc.),　Kunio Hisada,Motonari Mano, Hiromu Kuroda
(GK Graphics Inc.) 加藤完治　入江寿彦　西潟眞佐子（GK設計）　久田邦夫　真野元成　黒田 拓（GKグラフィックス）
DF: GK Sekkei Inc., GK Graphics Inc.　GK設計　GKグラフィックス　CO: Tanseisha Co., Ltd. (Sign), Nomura Co., Ltd. (IT
Sign) 丹青社（サイン）　乃村工藝社（ITサイン）　Symbol Mark Design: Takuya Onuki　大貫卓也　Pictogram Design
Partner: Kenzo Nagkagawa (NDC Graphics) 中川憲造（NDCグラフィックス）　SB: GK Sekkei Inc.　GK設計　JAPAN 2005

The concept for the signage plan was "a 3R design", i.e. REDUCE modifications to the natural environment resulting from the construction of foundations, etc. by rolling out mobile convertible scenery; REUSE materials by making it easier to dismantle, repair, replace, and reinstall equipment in different places, and ensure materials can be RECYCLEd separately. The emphasis was on eco-design, for example using materials such as biodegradable plastic film and bamboo laminate, and installing solar batteries and LED lighting.

サイン計画のコンセプトは「3Rからのデザイン」。これは可動可変な道具的展開によって、基礎工事など自然環境の改変抑制（Reduce）、分解・補修・部品交換・移設が容易（Reuse）、異素材ごとのリサイクル性を確保（Recycle）といった特性を持つ。生分解性樹脂幕、竹の集成材などの素材を用い、太陽電池とLED照明の設定などエコデザインを重視。

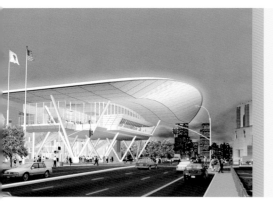

Boston Convention and Exhibition Center

Convention Center コンベンションセンター

CL: Massachusetts Convention Center Authority
S: Howard Davis
PR, DD: Stuart Ash
PC: Chris Herringer
D: Chris Herringer, Udo Schliemann, Terry Heard, Jonathan Picklyk, Jamie Cheung
P: Peter Garran
DF, SB: Gottschalk+Ash International
AR: HNTB and Rafael Vinoly Architects   P(ss): Peter Garran

USA 2004

The Boston Convention & Exhibition Center is the largest such facility in the Northeast. It opened in spring 2004 and has since become a landmark and symbol of the new Boston. The wayfinding system was custom designed to be compatible with the architectural language of the building. Based on the aluminum extrusion forming the main structural element, extruded outrigger brackets support anti-reflective glass sign panels. The building is color coded to enhance orientation.

ボストン・コンベンション&エキシビション・センターは米国北東部最大の催事施設。2004年のオープン以来、周辺のランドマークとなっている。経路案内システムは建築要素にそって設計。建築の主要素であるアルミ製の突き出しに合わせ、反射防止加工ガラスのサインパネルを張り出し型取付金具に設置。施設内の位置案内は色分けで実施。

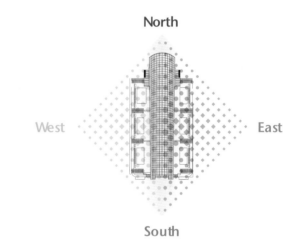

Sydney Exhibition and Convention Center

Convention Center　コンベンションセンター

CL, PC: Sydney Harbour Foreshore Authority (SHFA)
PC: SHFA
DD: Carlo Giannasca
D: Carlo Giannasca, Joanna Mackenzie, Paula Yu
DF, P(ss), SB: Frost Design, Sydney
CO: Claude Group

AUSTRALIA 2005

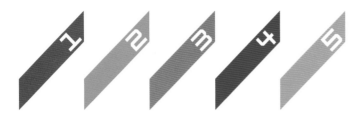

The Sydney Exhibition and Convention Centre commissioned a new signage system when it discovered visitors having trouble locating entrances. The solution: a series of "unmissable" nine-meter totems that act as giant pointers and a bold color scheme inspired by the Australian landscape to add impact. The totems also function at close range: each incorporates a lightbox unit for promoting events at the venue and an electronic messaging system enabling the Centre to deliver up-to-the minute information to visitors "on the ground".

この施設では訪問客が入口を探しにくいことがわかり、新サインシステムを導入。「見逃しようもない」ほど目立つ高さ9mのポールとオーストラリアの景色から着想を得た大胆な配色で、強い印象を与える方法がとられた。各ポールは会場のイベントを宣伝できるライトボックスを内蔵。Eメールシステムで「場内にいる」訪問客へ最新情報を配信することもできる。

Canadian War Museum

Museum　博物館

CL: Moriyama+Teshima Architects
S: Steve Dewingaerde
Producer of Signage: King Products
PC (for King): Matt Gillas
DD: Andrew Kuzyk　D: Andrew Kuzyk, John Pereira
DF, SB: Entro Communications
CO: PCL　AR: Moriyama+Teshima and Griffiths Rankin Cook
P(ss): Adrian Searce

CANADA　2005

The building has been designed to tell a powerful story of war, conflict, pain, and regeneration. Loosely based on a "tank countermeasure", directional slats placed at skewed angles suggest a war-torn environment, sign arrows resemble military stripes, and the stencil font is derived from CWM's corporate font, mimicking combat messages. Yellow text resembles zinc primer found on all military aircraft and the copper patina finish symbolizes regeneration.

戦争の生々しい情報や論争・苦痛・再生を伝えるための施設。若干、斜めを向いた方向指示板は「戦場」を意識し、戦争で荒廃した環境を暗示。標識の矢印は軍隊の縞模様を、当博物館の企業フォントをベースにしたステンシル・フォントは軍の通達を真似ている。黄色の文字は軍用機に使われる亜鉛下地剤を模したもので、銅の青サビ仕上げは再生を象徴。

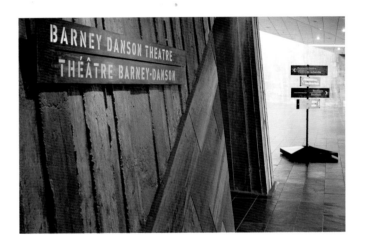

The Museum of Contemporary Arts

Museum　ミュージアム

CL: Belgiums' French Community
S, PC, DD: Jacques Bodelle
PR, DF, SB: ÉO Design Partners s.a.
D: Corinne Demaet, Christine Maniet
CO: Jean Vandervelde s.p.r.l.
P(ss): Yvan Glavie

BELGIUM 2004

The Museum of Contemporary Arts of the French Community - MAC is situated on a one of Europe's major industrial archeological site, the Grand Hornu. The signage had to integrate fully with the architecture of both the restored buildings and the new construction, and yet have a strong identity of its own. For the most part, the signage is applied directly to the concrete or walls without any intermediate support.

フランス・コミュニティ内の現代美術館MCAは有名なヨーロッパ産業の考古学的な史跡グラン・オルニュに併設されている。そのサインは改修された建物と新しい建築物の両方に合うものであると同時に強い印象を放つ必要があった。サインのほとんどはコンクリートや壁との間に支持具を使わず、直接取りつけられた。

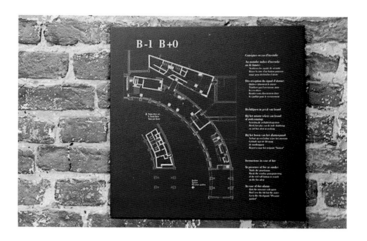

The National Museum of Modern Art, Tokyo
東京国立近代美術館

Museum 美術館

CL: Ministry of Land. Infrastructure and Transport Kanto Regional Development Bureau, The National Museum of Modern Art, Tokyo 国土交通省関東地方整備局 東京国立近代美術館
S, AR: Sakakura Associates 坂倉建築研究所 DD: Taro Watanabe (Emotional Space Design Inc.)
渡辺太郎（エモーショナル・スペース・デザイン） D: Kiriko Watanabe (Emotional Space Design Inc.)
渡辺希理子（エモーショナル・スペース・デザイン） P: Nacása & Partners Inc. ナカサアンドパートナーズ
CO: Kotobuki Corporation コトブキ SB: Emotional Space Design Inc. エモーショナル・スペース・デザイン

JAPAN 2002

Today, with a growing focus on the need for greater cultural input in our everyday lives, the public service function of art museums is again on the agenda. This was a signage plan for the National Museum of Modern Art, Tokyo, which accordingly wished to revive its function as an art museum responding proactively to the demands of the community. The idea was to design signage that would function as a spatial element integrated in a balanced manner, supplying information where it is wanted without being overly intrusive.

文化的な豊かさが問われる社会へと変化しつつある現代、改めて美術館の公共性が問われている。そうした積極的に社会の要請に応える美術館機能の今日的な再生を図った東京国立美術館のサイン計画。情報を知りたい場所で、その情報がノイズにならないよう、空間構成要素の一つとして機能し、バランスよく統合化されたサイン計画を目指した。

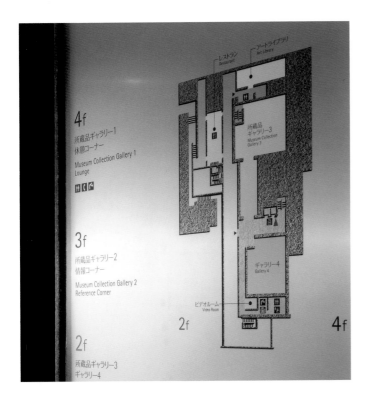

Art Gallery of Hamilton

Art Gallery アートギャラリー

CL: Art Gallery of Hamilton
S: Louise Dompierre, President and CEO
PC: Justin Young
DD: Udo Schliemann
DF, SB: Gottschalk+Ash International
CO: Sunset Neon Signs
AR: Kuwabara Payne McKennna Blumberg (KPMB) Architects
P(ss): Mike Lalich, Tom Arban

CANADA 2005

As part of a major gallery redevelopment signage, wayfinding and identity elements are critical components in making the gallery a more accessible and usable institution for visitors and an important ingredient in establishing a new image for the building. The major marquee identity element cantilevers from many blocks to the west of the gallery.

ギャラリーの大規模なサイン再開発プロジェクトでは、訪問客を当ギャラリーに来館しやすく、利用しやすくすることと、建物の新しいイメージを構築するうえで経路案内とVIが重要な要素となった。ギャラリー名を示す大きなサインは、建物西側の何ブロックも先から確認することができる。

National Museum of Australia

Museum 博物館

CL: National Museum of Australia
PR, PC, CO: Signcorp
DD: Steven Joseph
D: Nicky Hardcastle
DF, SB: Spatchurst

AUSTRALIA 2001

Spatchurst were the designers of the interior signage on the team commissioned to develop wayfinding strategy, signage design and documentation for the new compelling, controversial and anti-monumental museum. The form of the signage is designed to complement the Museum's interior architecture, which is characterized by organic shapes, vivid colors, and unexpected angles and textures.

Spatchurstは、記念碑的ではないが魅力のある話題の新博物館のための経路案内システム、サインデザイン、資料整理システムの開発を担当した屋内サインのデザインチーム。この博物館の内装は、有機的な形、鮮明な色彩、思いがけない角度やテクスチャーが特徴的。サインデザインはこれを補完するものが目指された。

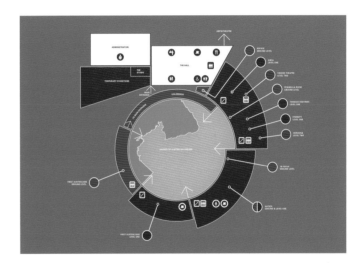

The National Museum of Australia's entrance and loop. Photo: John Gollings

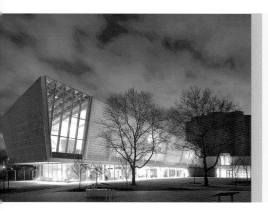

New York Hall of Science

Museum 科学館

CL, AR: Polshek Partnership Architects
D: L.Richard Poulin
DF, SB: Poulin+Morris Inc.
P(ss): Jeff Totaro

USA 2005

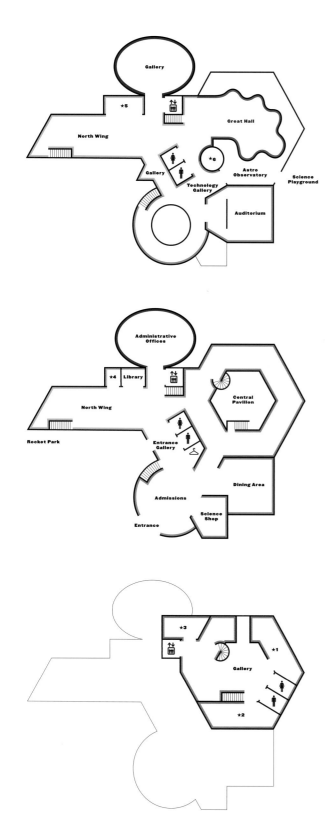

The expanded "Hall of Light" is intended to welcome and inspire curiosity in visitors. Sharing a similar objective, and because the Hall's exhibitions and programs are geared primarily towards children, teachers, and families, the signage system and environmental graphics rely on vivid colors, bold typography, floor patterns, and a series of symbolic geometric and organic sign shapes to convey a sense of playfulness, as well as function as a clear and iconographic wayfinding devices for the visitor.

広々とした光のホールや館内サイン、環境グラフィックは、訪問者を歓迎するとともに、好奇心を刺激するためにつくられた。科学館の展覧会やプログラムは、主に子ども、教師、家族を対象としているため、鮮やかな色彩、明瞭なタイポグラフィ、フロアパターンが用いられ、幾何学的かつ有機的なサインの形も象徴的なものが採用された。アイコンを使った明確なウェイファインディングとしての機能を果たしつつ、楽しさを感じさせる。

Zoom Children Museum

Museum　ミュージアム

CL: Zoom Children Museum
PR: Karas, Werbewerkstatt - Stefan Meszlenyi
PC: Monika Rosenkranz
DD, D: Erwin K. Bauer
P: Erwin K. Bauer, Herta Hurnaus
DF, CO, SB: Bauer-Concept & Design
AR: Pool

AUSTRIA　2003

Zoom is the main attraction in Vienna's the cultural district for families with kids. The orientation system is based on icons symbolizing the different sections. The large symbols are applied directly to walls or integrated in the furniture as back-lit glass elements. Thus the visual information melds with the architecture, and is visible from a distance. Detailed information appears on screens, integrated in the furniture above ticket and infopoints.

ズームはウィーンの文化地区にある、子ども連れ家族に人気の高い施設。案内システムでは様々なエリアをアイコンで表示。大きな記号を壁に直接貼ったり、バックライト付きガラスのような什器に取りつけたことで、視覚情報が建物に溶け込むと同時に遠くからでも確認可能に。チケット売場やインフォメーションの上に設置されたスクリーンは詳細情報を表示。

Jewish Children's Museum

Museum　ミュージアム

CL: Jewish Children's Museum
DD: Clifford Selbert
D: John Seeley, Marie Horchler, Greg Welch, Joe Kowan, Patrick Grey
DF, SB: Selbert Perkins Design
AR: Gwathmey Siegal and Associates, New York
P(ss): Esto Photography

USA　2004

Environmental graphics for a children's museum in New York, including identity, wayfinding and public art.

ニューヨークの子ども向けミュージアムの環境グラフィックス。VI、経路案内、公共芸術作品が制作された。

Miami Children's Museum

Museum ミュージアム

CL: Miami Children's Museum
DD: Robin Perkins
D: Erin Carney, Georgia Robrecht
DF, SB: Selbert Perkins Design
AR: Lee H. Skolnik Architecture
P(ss): Dana Bowden

USA 2004

Information graphics designed to seamlessly integrate with the interactive exhibits at the Miami Children's Museum in Miami, Florida. The graphics create a thematic, dynamic, and fun environment.

フロリダ、マイアミにあるマイアミ子ども博物館のインタラクティブな展示物にぴったりとフィットするようデザインされた情報グラフィックス。グラフィックスが、わかりやすいうえにダイナミックで楽しい環境を創り出している。

The National Museum of Art, Osaka　国立国際美術館

Museum　美術館

CL: Ministry of Land, Infranstructure and transport Kinki Regional Development Bureau
国土交通省 近畿地方整備局 独立行政法人国立美術館 国立国際美術館
DF: Hiromura Design Office, F. Plus Inc.　廣村デザイン事務所　エフプラス
CO, SB: Kotobuki Corporation　コトブキ
AR: Cesar Pelli & Associates Japan, Inc.　シーザーペリアンドアソシエーツジャパン
P(ss): Tokuaki Takimoto　滝本徳明

JAPAN 2004

Japan's first completely underground art museum, built in the center of Osaka's new culture hub. Being completely underground, the space needed to be created so that visitors would not lose their sense of direction. The design centers on an open cathedral-type ceiling, the result being an easy-to-understand, circulation-oriented structure supported by a simple signage program.

大阪の新たな芸術文化の中心地に建設された、日本初の完全地下型美術館。地下空間でありながら、方向性を見失わない空間を実現するため、吹き抜けを中心に設計された建築空間の分かりやすい動線計画を、シンプルなサインがサポートしている。

INDEX

SUBMITTER LIST

GUIDE SIGN GRAPHICS
ガイドサイングラフィックス

DESIGNER / デザイナー
CÉLIA SAYURI TAKAMATSU　高松セリアサユリ

JACKET DESIGN / ジャケットデザイン
HAJIME KABUTOYA　甲谷 一

EDITOR / 編集
SAECO OIKAWA　及川さえ子

WRITER / ライター
AYUKO ISHIBASHI　石橋亞由子

COORDINATORS / コーディネーター
MIKIKO SHIRAKURA　白倉三紀子
YASUKO TANIDA　谷田靖子
MARIKO ADACHI　安達万里子
NOZOMI KATO　加藤 希

TRANSLATORS / 翻訳
PAMELA MIKI　パメラ・ミキ
MARIAN KINOSHITA　木下マリアン
YUKO WADA　和田侑子
TAKAKO TSUKAGOSHI　塚越貴子
MIKIKO SHIRAKURA　白倉三紀子

PUBLISHER / 発行者
SHINGO MIYOSHI　三芳伸吾

2006年5月11日　初版第1刷発行

PIE BOOKS
2-32-4 MINAMI-OTSUKA, TOSHIMA-KU, TOKYO 170-0005 JAPAN
TEL: +81-3-5395-4811　FAX: +81-3-5395-4812
E-mail:　sales@piebooks.com
　　　　editor@piebooks.com
http://www.piebooks.com

発行所：ピエ・ブックス
〒170-0005　東京都豊島区南大塚2-32-4
編集　Tel: 03-5395-4820　Fax: 03-5395-4821
　　　E-mail: editor@piebooks.com
営業　Tel: 03-5395-4811　Fax: 03-5395-4812
　　　E-mail: sales@piebooks.com

印刷・製本　株式会社サンニチ印刷